FIRE's GUIDE TO
DUE PROCESS AND
FAIR PROCEDURE
ON CAMPUS

FIRE's GUIDES TO
STUDENT RIGHTS ON CAMPUS
www.thefire.org/guides

FIRE's Guide to Religious Liberty on Campus

FIRE's Guide to Student Fees, Funding, and Legal Equality
on Campus

FIRE's Guide to Due Process and Fair Procedure on Campus

FIRE's Guide to Free Speech on Campus

FIRE's Guide to First-Year Orientation and
to Thought Reform on Campus

FIRE

FIRE's GUIDE TO

DUE PROCESS AND FAIR PROCEDURE ON CAMPUS

Harvey A. Silverglate
Josh Gewolb

FOUNDATION FOR INDIVIDUAL RIGHTS IN EDUCATION
Philadelphia

This printing of FIRE's *Guide to Due Process and Fair Procedure on Campus* is made possible by a grant from the Claude R. Lambe Charitable Foundation. The Foundation for Individual Rights in Education gratefully acknowledges its support.

FIRE invites and welcomes requests for reproduction and retransmission of this publication. Contact: guides@thefire.org

   FIRE's guide to due process and fair procedure on campus / Harvey A. Silverglate & Josh Gewolb.
   p. cm.
 ISBN 0-9724712-2-7 (alk. paper)
 1. College students--Civil rights--United States. 2. College students--Legal status, laws, etc.--United States. 3. Universities and colleges--Law and legislation--United States. 4. Due process of law--United States. I. Title: Guide to due process and fair procedure on campus. II. Gewolb, Josh. III. Foundation for Individual Rights in Education. IV. Title.
 KF4243.S57 2003
 344.73'079--dc21

Published in the United States of America by:

           Foundation for Individual Rights in Education
           601 Walnut Street, Suite 510
           Philadelphia, PA 19106

Cover and interior design by Eliz. Anne O'Donnell

Printed in the United States of America

CONTENTS

Contents

PREFACE

Students should know their rights and liberties, and they need to be better informed and better equipped about how to assert and defend these precious things. The protectors of students' rights and liberties—those faculty, administrators, parents, alumni, friends, citizens, advisors, and attorneys who care about such vital matters—should understand the threats to freedom and legal equality on our campuses, the moral and legal means of combating those threats, and the acquired experience of recent years. To that end, the Foundation for Individual Rights in Education (FIRE) offers this *Guide to Due Process and Fair Procdure on Campus*, part of a series of such guides designed to restore individual rights and the values of a free society to our nation's colleges and universities. These guides also should remind those who write, revise, and enforce campus policies of the legal and moral constraints that restrict their authority. The sooner that colleges and universities understand their legal and moral obligations to a free and decent society, the less need there will be for guides such as these.

PART I: INTRODUCTION

This *Guide* is about what our culture has come to call "due process" or, more simply for most of us, fair procedure. In the course of many, many centuries, our civilization has evolved certain senses of what is proper or indecent, useful or harmful, right or wrong in the treatment of individuals faced with charges of wrongdoing. We have learned that one cannot separate **how** we reach decisions from the justice of those decisions, and, of course, from how confident we can be in the truth of those decisions. There were times when there was no presumption of innocence, no reasonable standard of proof, no right to impartial judges, no freedom to defend oneself appropriately, and, indeed, no prohibition against even torture and other processes that were the enemies of both justice and truth.

Some of the concepts in this *Guide* and some of the issues addressed may appear, at first glance, technical and dry—that is always a danger where the language of lawyers is unavoidable. The notions of due process, fundamental fairness, and fair procedure, however, touch the deepest issues of how we have learned to live together as decent human beings. If an innocent person is charged with wrongdoing, what protections should that innocent person have against being wrongly or arbitrarily punished and dishonored? If you or a loved one—your brother, sister, father, mother, or friend—had to face a tribunal and its rules, what expectations of fair procedure and the honest search for truth would you truly have? If you would not want yourself or a loved one tried in terrible ways, how could you bear seeing other people tried under those conditions? The level of fair process that a society, or any part of it, offers to individuals reflects its sense of decency and conscience. The issues discussed in this *Guide* touch upon the rules and learned lessons of civilized society. On a campus, as elsewhere, you have a moral right—and often a legal right—to decency and fundamental fairness. This *Guide* is about those rights. Behind the often legal language is a set of moral prin-

---

Definition: Due Process

An established course for judicial proceedings or other governmental activities designed to safeguard the legal rights of the individual.

--AMERICAN HERITAGE
DICTIONARY

---

ciples about how human beings may and may not treat each other.

If you face serious disciplinary action at a college or university, you are not alone. Many thousands of students come before campus courts each year, facing penalties that extend to suspension or expulsion. The bad news is that campus courts lack the kinds of basic fact-finding mechanisms and procedural safeguards that a decent society should provide, so you run a significant risk of being found responsible for a minor or, indeed, serious offense even if you are innocent. Furthermore, offenses that are considered relatively minor in the criminal justice system are sometimes categorized as major on campus and can lead to severe sanctions. The good news is that there is much that you can do to secure more fairness and to protect yourself and your future.

Fortunately, students facing disciplinary action at both public and private universities have certain rights. This guide is designed to help you understand these rights. The outcome of a disciplinary case should depend on whether you are factually guilty or innocent, not on the adequacy or inadequacy of a university's disciplinary processes. Campus administrators—frequently advised by the college's or university's lawyers or general counsel (an attorney who works specifically for the institution)—currently have a virtual monopoly on information about the legal requirements of campus judicial systems and procedures. We believe, however, that if you know your legal rights—and, where necessary, let your institution know that you will exercise them—you can be accorded a greater degree of procedural fairness. We believe as well that students facing disciplinary tribunals should develop specific skills in preparing a defense.

How to Use This Guide

This *Guide* is intended both to help accused students understand the procedural safeguards to which they are entitled and to give them tactical advice on how to secure these protections.

Part I explains what due process is and the reason it is so important to a free and decent society. Part II discusses due process at public universities in a general way. Part III describes the ways in which the law guarantees fair procedures at private universities. Finally, Part IV goes into more detail about the specific procedural protections to which students at a public university are entitled.

This *Guide* does not take up, except broadly, the subject of how to prepare an effective defense. Every case is different, so it is not possible to make general recommendations about strategy. Our focus is on how you can gain the chance to be judged fairly.

Even if you have only a specific question, you should try to read the guide in its entirety. You may have rights that you may not be aware of, and using all of your rights is the best way to ensure a fair outcome in your case.

Your Rights If You Face Disciplinary Action

If you face possible significant punishment by a **public** college or university—expulsion, suspension, or some lesser but still significant sanction—you are entitled to certain rights under the Constitution's guarantee of "due process." (Learn the relevant terms, and use them. It truly makes a difference when administrators know that you understand your legal rights and can state them in legal or, at least, accurate, language. They suddenly wonder to whom you have been talking.) Think of due process as meaning "fair and regular procedures." Students facing serious penalties at a public university are entitled to have their case heard according to such "fair and regular procedures."

The disciplinary proceedings of public colleges and universities are governed by the United States Constitution, because state schools are governmental institutions. The Fifth and Fourteenth Amendments to the Constitution promise that the government will not deprive any person of "life, liberty, or property, without due process of law." This means that what lawyers call "accusatory proceedings" of any sort, including campus disciplinary proceedings, must be handled in a regularized manner—not in an arbitrary manner designed for this or that particular case—and must include procedural safeguards that match the seriousness of the potential punishment.

The specific procedural protection to which due process entitles you depends on your particular situation. In general, the more serious the charge and potential penalty, the greater the protections that must be given to you. This is why students in campus disciplinary cases are not entitled to as many rights as those found in the criminal justice system: imprisonment, for pretty good reason, is considered more serious than getting kicked out of school. That is why, in the legal system, traffic court offers fewer protections than a court that hears charges of a serious crime.

In any case involving suspension or expulsion for **disciplinary reasons** at a **public** university, you are entitled to the following protections:

- The right to have your case heard under regular procedures used for all similar cases
- The right to receive notice of the charges against you
- The right to hear a description of the university's evidence against you
- The right to present your side of the story to an impartial panel

You are entitled to the rights listed above in all cases involving disciplinary suspension or expulsion. In certain circumstances, as discussed in more detail in Part IV, you may also be entitled to other rights, such as the right to cross-examine witnesses or to retain a lawyer to assist in your defense.

These same rules do not apply, however, to students who face suspension or expulsion from even a public university because of poor **academic** performance. Very few procedural safeguards are required in academic dismissals, because the courts do not feel comfortable second-guessing academic judgments. All that due process requires in academic cases is that universities treat students in a manner that is careful and not arbitrary, and that students be given a reasonable opportunity to present their defense or explanation.

Unlike public universities, **private** universities, because they are not part of the government, are not legally required to offer students constitutional due process. However, private universities are frequently bound by contract law to follow their own established disciplinary processes. If a private university says that it will offer a certain safeguard, it is obliged to do so, more or less in the manner that any private party entering into a contract with another party would be obliged to fulfill that agreement. Breach of contract is both a moral and a legal wrong.

Public universities also are bound by contract law to follow their own rules. If a public university promises greater procedural protections than due process requires, it must actually give them to you. We spend much of this guide describing the minimal procedural protections guaranteed by due process, but in fact, the actual issue, in many cases, is the university's promise to go beyond these rights. Promises matter, and students have considerable power in holding universities to their promises.

Finally, **both** public and private universities are bound by federal laws that guarantee the privacy of student disciplinary records. These laws, for example, govern whether or not universities may report disciplinary convictions to the police or talk about them with the news media. Though these particular privacy laws are not a part of due process, we briefly discuss them because they provide important protections to students accused of misconduct.

How to Approach Your Disciplinary Case

If you have done (or are suspected of having done) something that you believe might lead to a disciplinary proceeding, you should promptly read your campus's disciplinary rules and procedures even before you are charged. You can usually find these rules on your university website or in your student handbook. You need to know certain things before the process begins. How will you be notified if you are charged? How long will you

CRIME, EDUCATION, AND PUNISHMENT

College and university administrators often argue that campus discipline is "educational" rather than punitive, and that instituting "formal procedures" or "legalistic protections" is inappropriate because of the educational character of the disciplinary process. This argument ignores the fact that, in serious cases, campus justice is truly punitive, not gentle. Expulsion from a university can be life-altering. Suspensions, and other punishments that disrupt a student's education, can be very serious events in life. These sanctions are often imposed for offenses that would be very minor in the nonuniversity criminal justice system. All punishment is necessarily educational in some sense, since people are supposed to learn a lesson from being punished, but this does not detract from the need for fair procedures to make sure that only the guilty are disciplined. Procedural protections exist in our society because history has proven that without them, people who have power will abuse the rights of the powerless and that many innocent people will be hurt in the process.

have to prepare your defense? What opportunity will you have to present your case? Does your university offer more rights and protections than the minimal requirements set by due process?

Once you understand the university's rules, you can begin to plan your defense. Interview witnesses and collect evidence that may help you fight the charges. It is important to begin your defense as early as possible—and certainly as soon as you receive notice that you have been charged—especially if your university offers only a brief time within which to try disciplinary cases. Evidence and memories are at their freshest soon after an event.

Many students ask if they should retain a lawyer to help fight disciplinary charges. The answer, predictably, depends on the circumstances. If you think that you may be charged criminally for the same conduct that led to your disciplinary case, it is absolutely crucial to have an attorney. Anything that you say to the university's disciplinary committee can be used against you in criminal court, so you should consult a lawyer before making any statements whatsoever. On the other hand, if it is unlikely that you will also face criminal charges, it is really up to you whether or not to retain legal counsel. Having a competent lawyer certainly can't hurt you, but other people at your college, such as informed and sympathetic professors or residence advisors, may actually have more experience with the disciplinary process than nonuniversity attorneys—and they will almost always work free of charge. Be careful, though. Campus advisors—especially administrators—may well have a conflict of interest. Their primary loyalty, personally and, often, legally, may be to the university rather than to you.

How to Fight for Fair Treatment

This guide often discusses students who sue their universities to obtain due process. The reason for this is that the law of due process has emerged from the accumulated decisions of the courts in past legal cases, which are known as **precedents**. Talking about these legal cases is the best way to describe the current state of student due process rights.

However, discussion of past legal cases is not intended to suggest that it is necessarily a good idea for you to file a lawsuit in your particular case. In fact, only a handful of disciplinary cases ever reach the point where it would be reasonable to file suit. Even in cases where lawsuits are possible, they are often a bad idea. These suits can last many years and cost thousands of dollars, and often your biggest gain is simply a new hearing. That new hearing might allow you to present evidence and to make your arguments in fairer circumstances, but it will not necessarily achieve your vindication. On the other hand, if the university's mistreatment of you has been outrageous, if the evidence of your innocence is strong but ignored, and if the precedents in your judicial district are favorable to students' rights, a lawsuit might indeed be a realistic alternative.

Court Decisions About School Discipline Differ by Place

This guide refers to cases decided by many different courts. Technically, the rulings of a court are binding only on future cases in the same court (or in a lower court in the same geographic area). Opinions of the United States Supreme Court are the only cases binding throughout the entire country. It would be ideal, of course, if you (or your lawyer) found that your college was in a jurisdiction with a useful precedent. Most of the time, however, you will need to rely on the persuasive value of the decisions we describe, not on their binding authority.

Sometimes you can get the added procedural protections you need just by asking for them. If you believe that the disciplinary procedures used by your university are preventing you from mounting an effective defense, you should explain the problem to the responsible administrators. For example, if the university gives you only ten days notice of the date of your disciplinary hearing, and you have a busy schedule, an illness, or pressing personal or family obligations during that period, you should simply talk to the administrators and explain the problem to them. It is usually best, at first, to appeal to reason, common sense, and basic notions of fairness, rather than to legal rules. In many cases, the administration will accommodate your request. In order to create a written record of an oral request, it is very important to follow up a discussion with a polite and informal letter or e-mail, restating both what you asked for and the reasons for your request. (Using e-mail to correspond with those involved in the disciplinary process makes it easy to document your requests and discussions, without making it quite so obvious that you are keeping such a written record.)

There are two things that you can do if the university refuses to grant your request. First, submit a written letter, to the appropriate administrator or administrators, about what you would have shown if the safeguard you requested had been granted. For example, if the university tells you that you may not speak to a crucial witness during your investigation, you should submit a statement in writing about what this interview, if allowed to proceed, would have shown. For one thing, that statement will be part of the record, and the fact-finders may manage to see it anyway. For another, if you later do have to go to court, the judge will see clearly what you could have proven given a fair opportunity.

Second, if you think that you are being a denied a protection that is critical to your case, consider a threat, indirect or direct, of legal action. Many students find that it is most effective to suggest subtly, before any suit, the possibility of legal action. Informally tell the administrators responsible for your case that you believe the university's disciplinary procedures to be unlawful and explain why (with language taken from this guide). Administrators live in fear of powerful lawsuits, and this mere hint of legal action may be enough to earn you the protections you wish.

If this informal approach fails, you can formally threaten legal action in writing. If you have a good basis

---

FIVE STEPS TO DEFENDING YOURSELF

When faced with a disciplinary charge:

1. Carefully read your student handbook, disciplinary code, and other campus policies that apply to you or to your organization.

2. Read this guide in its entirety and then re-read the sections most applicable to your case and to your type of university.

3. Take careful notes of conversations. Send e-mails that restate the conversations that you have had. Keep copies of any written correspondence with administrators, faculty members, or student leaders.

4. Obtain an advisor or lawyer who can help you navigate the disciplinary process.

5. Give your disciplinary hearing first priority and prepare for it well in advance.

---

for a lawsuit and threaten to bring one, the administration may well back down. Colleges often find it wiser to settle **before** a lawsuit is filed rather than face legal fees, wasted time, the embarrassment of a public record of their unfairness, and the possibility of creating a bad legal precedent for themselves. The university may step back when you let it know that it is violating the law, making it unnecessary for you to take the final step of securing legal counsel and filing suit.

If requests and demands for due process and threats to sue fail, and if you have the facts and the law on your side, you can indeed sue your university. As noted above, however, such lawsuits can be very difficult and extremely expensive. College administrators might compromise or settle with you fairly early. However, they might not, and universities usually get "free" legal representation from the state or from their general counsel (that is, paid by either taxpayers or student tuitions), so they have a financial advantage over you for the long haul. If your case presents an important issue, however, you may be able to obtain skilled and free representation from a variety of civil liberties organizations and legal foundations.

PART II: DUE PROCESS AT PUBLIC UNIVERSITIES

Due Process in American Law

If you want to wield your due process rights to maximum advantage, you should have a basic understanding of 1) due process in the nonuniversity criminal justice system and 2) the legal and moral theories behind the ways due process does and does not apply to college disciplinary procedures.

Due process has evolved over the centuries as a way to ensure that accusatory proceedings produce accurate and truthful results. This is one of the most vital components of a free, decent, and fair society. The Anglo-American experience has taught us that the procedures of due process (the process that is "due" or "owed" to each citizen) are essential to ensure the best chance of learning the truth during the trial process. Juries stand the best chance of getting to the bottom of complicated factual matters if, for example, the accused is allowed to be in the same room as his accuser, and if the accused's lawyer is given an opportunity to ask probing questions of the accuser and of hostile witnesses. How comfortable does an accusing witness appear as he or she looks the accused in the eye and testifies? How credibly does the accusing witness respond to hard questions put by a skilled cross-examiner? These are not "technicalities," but, rather, the stuff of fair decisions and justice. The jurisprudence of due process is greatly concerned with identifying specific procedures that are actually effective in discovering the truth.

Procedural Due Process

Procedural due process (a legal term) refers to the rules that govern how an accusatory proceeding is carried out—the steps by which a matter is "tried" in order to determine the truth or falsity of an accusation. Examples of procedural due process might include the rules governing the defendants' rights to question witnesses who testify against them and to be tried by a jury of their peers. The use of these procedures reflects society's solemn commitment to the importance of obtaining an accurate result when a citizen stands accused. (While the rights of most interest to you as a student accused of a disciplinary infraction are those of **procedural** due process, due process also confers another set of rights, known as **substantive** due process rights, which are defined and discussed in Part IV, Section I.)

The right to procedural due process in contemporary America comes from the Fifth and Fourteenth Amendments to the United States Constitution. The Fifth Amendment's due process requirement acts as a limit on the power of **federal** government and its institutions, while the Fourteenth Amendment's due process restricts the power of **state** governments. As a practical matter, most of the restrictions on the federal government's power over the rights of citizens also apply, through the Fourteenth Amendment, to state government. These constitutional provisions guarantee that the federal and state governments, respectively, may not deprive any person "of life, liberty, or property, without due process of law." Your interest in your diploma and in the value of a clear academic record establishes a property right. Your interest in your reputation and good name establishes a liberty right.

Each of the tens of thousands of court opinions that have interpreted these constitutional guarantees proceeds basically in a simple two-step manner:

First, the court looks to see whether due process applies—that is, whether a person's life, liberty, or property is being put at risk because of something the government is doing.

Second, if the person is entitled to due process, the court determines what process actually is due under the particular circumstances.

Due process is flexible. The process that is due depends largely on the context. As the United States Supreme Court held in *Mathews v. Eldridge* (1976), courts must consider three factors to see whether a particular protection is required in a given situation:

1. What is at stake for the person?

2. How risky is it that under the current procedures the person will be wrongly punished and how likely is it that more safeguards would reduce the risk?

3. How costly and time consuming would the new protections be for the government?

Some situations clearly require the most protective due process, such as the criminal trial of a person on a serious charge such as murder, which may result in the defendant's being deprived of liberty or even life. Other situations, including civil cases and charges brought against students in disciplinary tribunals of public colleges and universities, require a different—and much less elaborate—level of procedural protections. Still other situations, such as the suspension or expulsion of a student for poor academic performance, require even fewer safeguards.

Procedural Protections in Disciplinary Cases

University officials often say that since college disciplinary proceedings are "educational" rather than punitive, students in such proceedings are not entitled to procedural protections. The law, however, is clear that protections of due process are in fact required for disciplinary hearings at public universities.

This is the case because, as noted above, people are entitled to due process rights whenever they have what are known as "liberty" or "property" interests at stake. Both interests are most certainly at stake in university disciplinary hearings.

LIBERTY AND PROPERTY INTERESTS

The United States Supreme Court has held that "liberty interests" are involved (lawyers would say "implicated") whenever a person's good name, reputation, honor, or integrity is at stake. The tarnishing of a student's reputation by a disciplinary board can have a devastating effect on his or her future education and career. An expulsion from college may not be as serious as a prison sentence in terms of deprivation of liberty, but there is no question that it can have a profound impact on the rest of a student's life.

The progress that a student has made toward a degree constitutes property—a thing of value that belongs to a person—because of all the time and money that he or she has invested in this education. Once the state has chosen to grant students a property right by admitting them to an institution of higher education, it cannot revoke this right arbitrarily or unfairly.

Students facing disciplinary hearings at public colleges and universities, thus, have **both** liberty and property interests at stake.

The more serious the possible deprivations of liberty and property—generally, the more serious the accusation—the greater the kind of due process, with more substantial procedural protections, that is required. Most of our discussion focuses on the protections due to students facing possible suspension or expulsion, but liberty and property are also at stake in cases involving more minor potential punishments. Students are entitled to a different kind of due process, with fewer procedural protections, however, in cases involving only minor sanctions. There are some cases where the potential deprivations of liberty and property are so minor that very little or no process is due. The courts have not laid out precisely where this threshold lies in the university context. This is an area of law very much in development and formation.

Disciplinary Cases Involving Suspension or Expulsion

Students facing possible suspension or expulsion from public colleges and universities are entitled to due process because liberty and property are clearly at stake. This raises the question of precisely **what** process is due. As noted, because the liberty and property interests involved in suspension or expulsion from institutions of higher education are much smaller than those posed by criminal conviction, less procedural protection is required in a campus tribunal than in a court of criminal law.

The consensus established by the courts is that, at the absolute minimum, students in campus disciplinary cases are entitled to have **notice of the charges against them**, a **disclosure or explanation of the evidence** behind the charges, and an **opportunity to contest** this evidence.

The United States Supreme Court established these minimal requirements in *Goss v. Lopez* (1975), where nine suspended Ohio high school students sued their school, claiming that they had been denied due process. The Court, weighing the costs and benefits to the school and to the students, held that although the most severe suspensions were only ten days long, the students had constitutional rights protected by the due process clause of the Fourteenth Amendment. The Court ruled that in student disciplinary cases involving short suspensions, an accused student must be "given oral or written notice of the charges against him and, if he denies them, an explanation of the evidence the authorities have and an opportunity to present his side of the story." The Court held that, at the very least, administrators must engage in an "informal give-and-take" with a student immediately after an incident of alleged misconduct and before

Isn't *Goss* a High School Case?

It is. Typically, however, courts have held that students in higher education are entitled to **more** procedural protections than students in the lower grades, because college students are adults in the eyes of the law. As a university student, you certainly need to consult **university** cases to understand the full scope of your rights. High school cases are very useful to you too, however, because as a college student you have **at least** the same rights accorded to high school students. Further, because there are more high school than college students, high school jurisprudence may be better developed on the point at issue in your case. Thus, secondary school legal precedents establish a **floor**, but **not** a ceiling to the rights accorded a college student.

imposing a penalty. However, the Court specifically stated that administrators may wish, in more difficult cases, to permit counsel, to hold hearings, or to allow cross-examination.

Although, to a certain extent, *Goss* left the decision of whether to offer these greater protections to the "discretion" of administrators, it also stated that due process "may require more formal procedures" in more serious cases. Since *Goss*, the lower federal courts and various state courts have wrestled on a case-by-case basis with the issue of when such requirements apply. (There has been no higher court decision to clarify things more generally.) The principle firmly established by these federal and state courts is that the amount of due process required in campus disciplinary cases must be based on the particular nature and gravity of the charges and circumstances.

Exactly what protections are required in particular cases, however, remains unsettled. Courts have allowed protections such as cross-examination and the right to an attorney in cases where they have judged these safeguards to be critical to basic fairness, but they have denied them in other cases where they believed that students could get a just hearing without such extra protections.

The most general statement that can be made is that judges must weigh the costs and benefits, for the institution and for the parties involved, in each particular case.

In considering the cost of more elaborate procedures or new procedural safeguards—in terms of time, effort, money, and interference with the smooth running of the university—that cost must be balanced against the likelihood of grave error or injustice if the procedural safeguard were not offered.

Under this analysis, many courts insist on stricter procedural protections in cases involving or even touching upon freedom of speech. Constitutionally protected vital rights are the foundation of our liberty, and when they are at stake, the need for fair procedure is at its most critical.

Several factors keep the courts from establishing more specific rules. First, due process by its very nature is supposed to be flexible. The establishment of one-size-fits-all rules would be contrary to the constitutional premise that one has a right only to the process that is "due." Second, only a small number of campus due process cases have reached the courts, and it would take more cases than those to smooth out the differences among how various jurisdictions treat the same situation. Third, the courts are generally very wary about interfering with the internal affairs of a college or university, seeing the freedom of campuses from government interference as essential to "academic freedom"—which can be loosely defined as the right of higher education to proceed in its teaching and its scholarship without government interference. No meaning of academic freedom, however, gives higher education the right to break the law.

Even though the law is unsettled and even a bit conflicted, it is still possible to get a general sense of how courts approach particular aspects of campus due process. Part IV of this guide reviews the state of the law with respect to particular procedural safeguards.

Procedural Protections in Pedagogical Cases

So far we have spoken only about disciplinary cases. Students who face suspension or expulsion because of poor academic performance are also entitled to due process. Only minimal protections are required, however. Universities must make academic decisions in a manner that is careful and not arbitrary, but they do not have to grant students any of the procedural safeguards required in disciplinary matters.

Fewer procedural protections are required in academic cases because the evaluation of academic merit rarely hinges on common facts but, rather, on subjective assessments of ability that professors, almost by definition, are better equipped to make than judges. The procedural protections of the criminal law are useful for fact-finding and therefore not required in cases involving subjective judgments of performance. A professor's grading of a student's academic performance is protected from court interference by the principle of academic freedom, unless the professor's assessment can be shown to have been influenced by improper factors, such as the student's race or political viewpoint.

The United States Supreme Court considered the balance, in academic expulsions, between academic freedom and due process in two major cases of the late 1970s and early 1980s. In *Board of Curators of the University of Missouri v. Horowitz* (1978), the Court reviewed a due process claim advanced by a student who was dismissed from a public medical school because of poor academic performance. The student was never given an opportunity to be heard by any of the university committees that took up her case. However, the Court held that hearings and associated procedural protections are not required in academic dismissal cases, because they do not involve the kind of factual determinations in which heightened protections would be useful. The Court ruled that Horowitz's treatment was consistent with due process because of a few basic conditions. Her academic work had been reviewed in a "careful and deliberate" manner by both faculty members and school committees; she had been given ample notice that her work was judged to be unsatisfactory; and she had been granted a number of chances to exhibit improvement.

The United States Supreme Court expanded on this in *Ewing v. University of Michigan* (1985), in which a student alleged that due process was denied when he was dismissed from a medical program after receiving the lowest score ever recorded on a standardized test in the history of that program. He complained that many other students with even poorer overall academic records had been allowed to retake the standardized test. In refusing to interfere with the expulsion, the Court invoked the principle of academic freedom. It ruled that courts should defer to universities' judgments on **academic matters** unless there is such a "substantial departure from accepted academic norms as to demonstrate that the person or committee responsible did not actually exercise professional judgment." Because the student's overall record was exceptionally poor, the university's decision to dismiss him was well within its discretion.

Lower courts have interpreted these decisions to require that colleges and universities make academic decisions in a manner that is "careful and deliberate," or at least not "arbitrary and capricious." Courts will intervene in academic decisions only if you were treated with gross unfairness or on the basis of prohibited factors and criteria.

If you made a clear case, however, that the academic sanctions against you were not based on reason or fact—or arose from other grudges held against you—you then might convince a court to set aside its presumption in favor of the university. For example, in *Vaksman v. Alcorn* (1994), the Court of Appeals of Texas ordered that a public university readmit an expelled graduate student. The court ruled that the dismissal was made on the basis of personal hostility arising from the student's intellectual disagreements with the faculty and his outspoken criticism of university policies—not on the basis of the student's erratic (but occasionally distinguished) academic record.

Additionally, courts have sometimes required that students be given advance notice that their poor performance has placed their status in jeopardy, or, failing that, be given notice of the general standard of performance expected of students.

Cheating: The Border Between Academic and Disciplinary Offenses

Cheating—the use of fraud or deception to enhance one's academic performance—stands at the boundary of academic and disciplinary realms.

Sometimes, for due process purposes, cases of cheating are clearly disciplinary cases, as, for instance, when a student copies from another student's paper by looking over his shoulder during an exam. Determining guilt or innocence in such cases is a matter of fact-finding: Did the student actually copy? If the facts indicate that a rule was broken, the student is guilty; if they do not, the student is innocent. The procedural protections of due process are designed to assist precisely these sorts of factual judgments.

In contrast, charges of plagiarism, a form of cheating, include both academic and disciplinary elements. On the one hand, the real question in a plagiarism case is whether or not you committed the particular act of using someone else's work without attribution. That is a factual question. On the other hand, the question of whether your words were so close to those of another, uncited source that your work constitutes plagiarism also requires skilled academic judgment. The issue to be resolved in a campus plagiarism case is thus both factual and judgmental.

When you seek a court's intervention, it is in your interest to define the charge as "disciplinary," offering you more safeguards, while it is in the interest of the school's administrators and lawyers to define the charge as "academic," offering them greater discretionary power. Sometimes that line is quite vague, as in the case of plagiarism. Having your case treated as disciplinary in the campus proceedings themselves would create a record that strengthens your argument in court that the case is indeed a disciplinary rather than an academic matter.

The University Must Deliver What It Promises

A public college or university may not decide on its own not to grant the due process rights that the Constitution requires. The Constitution mandates these rights. If your college or university denies you any of the protections required by due process, you can make a due process claim in federal or state court.

Many public colleges and universities, however, actually promise students considerably more than due process requires. The law does not oblige campuses to offer a full and formal judicial hearing, for example, but many universities provide something fairly close to one. The law does not always require campus tribunals to permit formal cross-examination of witnesses, but many universities themselves have chosen to allow for such cross-examination.

Courts will generally compel **public** universities to give you all of the procedural protections that they have promised. The courts enforce these obligations, however, not as a matter of your rights to due process, but as a right you have under state contract law. This same doctrine also binds **private** universities to follow their advertised or published disciplinary policies as discussed in Part III. Some states also have rules that require administrative agencies to follow their own regulations. If you live in such a state, these administrative rules may provide an additional legal theory useful to force a public university to obey its own rules.

The case of *Morrison v. University of Oregon Health Science Center* (1984), decided by the Court of Appeals of Oregon, illustrates the advantages of making a contract claim, rather than a due process claim, if your university deviates from the rules it established for itself. The issue was whether or not a university had followed its own procedures when it dismissed a dental student for academic reasons. The university's policy stated that only evidence raised at a student's actual hearing could be considered in reaching such a decision, but the record showed that the university had considered evidence never raised at this hearing. The court ordered the university to annul a dismissal that had been reached by a violation of its own promised procedures. This victory could not have been gained on due process grounds, because due process does not **require** universities to grant students a hearing in academic cases.

In sum, if your public college or university denies you basic procedural protections guaranteed by the Constitution, you may have a due process claim. If your public college or university fails to follow its own rules, you may have a claim under several other headings, including state doctrines about contract that oblige organizations to honor their own promises, a reasonable obligation indeed.

PART III:
PROCEDURAL FAIRNESS
AT PRIVATE UNIVERSITIES

Public universities, as an arm of the government, have to follow certain constitutionally required standards in setting rules and disciplining students. Private colleges or universities are free, by contrast, within very wide guidelines and boundaries established by state laws, to set their own rules and to formulate their own disciplinary procedures. A student is free to take or not to take such procedures into account when deciding to attend such an institution. Once private institutions establish and publish disciplinary rules, however, they are then obliged, by principles of contract law, to follow them in good faith, even if not always to the strict letter.

Private Universities Generally Must Follow Their Established Procedures

Private universities are not required to promise fair procedures to their students. However, nearly all universities have student handbooks and judicial manuals that set out rules and standards for their student judicial systems. Courts in many states have held that these rules and standards form a contract of sorts, and that universities must live up to them in at least a general way.

The legal requirement that universities actually give students the rights they promise stems from a variety of doctrines, above all from the law of contracts. The basic principle of contract law is also one that lies at the heart of morality: people have to live up to their reciprocal promises. If one party agrees to a contract and doesn't honor it, the court can force that party to do so and can award monetary damages to the other party. If you agree to attend a university and pay tuition and fees, and you do so relying at least in part upon the rules and regulations that the university tells you it has established, then a deal of sorts has been struck, roughly like a legal contract.

Courts have often held that the representations universities make in their student handbooks about the disciplinary process are promises that they must keep. However, courts do not enforce these promises as strictly as other kinds of contracts, which would be meticulously enforced. For example, the courts typically will not give students monetary damages when colleges simply fail to follow their disciplinary rules. In addition, they tend to give universities a certain leeway if they have followed their rules in a general way, even if not to the letter. The consensus of the courts is that the relationship between a student and a university has, as one judge put it, a "strong, albeit flexible, contractual flavor," and that the promises made in handbooks have to be "substantially observed."

Some states follow an ancient "common law" doctrine—not embodied in any statute but followed by courts on the basis of longstanding practice and precedent—that binds private organizations to treat their members with at least a minimal level of fairness and decency. This doctrine reinforces the contract law rules requiring universities to follow their own procedures.

While courts have not held that universities must adhere to their rules precisely, you can sometimes use the mere threat of a lawsuit to force your university to follow its own rules. Colleges and universities do indeed fear lawsuits when they are very likely in the wrong. If you make it clear that you know your rights, your university is less likely to stray too far from keeping its promises, thus placing itself in a gray area of possible breach of contract.

You also can use to your advantage the fact that your university itself set the terms of its student handbook.

When a contract, or a contract-like agreement, is formulated by what the law terms "the stronger party," and "the weaker party" does not have an opportunity to negotiate specific terms, courts will lean in favor of the weaker party in resolving any ambiguities in the contract. Under this standard—applied to higher education,

"DISCOVERY" AND CIVIL SUITS: UNIVERSITIES AND THE COURT OF PUBLIC OPINION

Another reason why universities fear credible lawsuits involves what the law terms "discovery," which occurs before the start of a civil trial. During discovery, the university must produce for your lawyer and the court all of the information relevant to your case. This can include e-mail, administrative correspondence, internal documents, or other evidence. Once this evidence is submitted, it usually becomes a public record. This information is not only essential to your legal case, but is often very embarrassing to the university when it reveals unfairness or even malice. Universities sometimes treat their own students in ways that they would be ashamed to reveal to the general public, even if their behavior possibly broke no laws. Therefore, universities are sometimes frightened of defending claims they well might win, when doing so would reveal that they acted in an unfair or outrageous manner.

for example, in the U.S. District Court for the District of Columbia case of *Giles v. Howard University* (1977)— courts will interpret rules in a student handbook with whatever meaning the university should reasonably expect **students** to give them.

Breach of Contract Lawsuits

If you sue your university for breach of contract, the court—in a jurisdiction with precedents favorable to student rights—will review the student handbook and the record of your trial, to see if the university failed to meet your reasonable expectations and therefore violated its contract with you.

Because most courts view the student handbook as having to be only what the law terms "substantially" (rather than precisely) observed, it is difficult to win a suit if the university can argue plausibly that it fulfilled its promises in some general way. For example, in the Massachusetts Supreme Judicial Court case of *Schaer v. Brandeis* (2000), a student sued Brandeis University for, among other things, failing to produce a "summary report" of his disciplinary hearing, as promised by the student handbook. Brandeis had summarized the five-hour hearing in a mere twelve lines of text. The Massachusetts Supreme Judicial Court ruled that although it would be a better practice to issue a more complete summary, Brandeis's published procedures never had stated precisely how detailed a summary it would produce. Therefore, the court held, the twelve-line summary did not break its promise to the student, although the better practice may have been to produce a more complete summary. Courts do not always reach decisions that most ordinary citizens would find fair.

However, when your university clearly has failed to live up to its obligations to you, then you have a genuine chance of obtaining judicial relief. For example, in the case of *Fellheimer v. Middlebury College* (1994), the U.S. District Court for the District of Vermont cleared the disciplinary record of a Middlebury College student who had been found innocent of rape by the campus court but who was instead convicted of "disrespect for persons." However, he had never even been notified that he was being prosecuted for **that** offense. Middlebury's handbook at the time promised that accused students would be told of the charges against them "with sufficient particularity to permit [them] to meet the charges." While Middlebury told Fellheimer that he was charged with rape, he was not told that he was also being charged with "disrespect for persons." He only learned about that second charge when he had been convicted of it. The court held that while Middlebury, a private college not bound by constitutional due process requirements, was under no general obligation to tell its students of the charges against them, it had nonetheless agreed to do so and had failed to live up to that promise in Fellheimer's case.

"This Is Not a Contract": University Disclaimers Are Invalid

Sadly, as the law increasingly has called upon our institutions of higher education to live up to their promises, campuses have sought new ways to be free from having to follow the rules that they advertise. Many universities, acting on the advice of their lawyers, now add disclaimers to their student manuals, stating that they are not required to adhere to them completely. Others state specifically that the procedures set forth in student handbooks should not be viewed by students as contractual promises. Middlebury's handbook in the Fellheimer case, for example, said that the procedures were only to be adhered to "as faithfully as possible." Such language may give universities additional leeway, but, as seen in the Middlebury case, it does not allow universities to ignore their own rules. Universities are less likely to cross the line into the gray area of what might be impermissible misconduct if they know that you are aware of your right to judicial relief should they cross that line.

The preamble to your university's disciplinary code may help make the case that this or that unfair practice violates your university's disciplinary rules, even where your university promises merely to follow its procedures "as faithfully as possible." Why? Many preambles assure "fundamental fairness" or "integrity and impartiality" in the administration of the campus court. Even if your university's handbook contains an escape clause ("as faithfully as possible"), you can make the strong case that the university was so deeply unfaithful to its own published rules that it broke its overarching promise to offer fair procedures.

Some colleges even state in their student handbooks that their own rules and even promises do not constitute a contract. Such claims are often not meaningful, and you should not let them fool you. Universities plainly intend their student handbooks to be read as a promise of fairness; such promises cannot reasonably be interpreted as meaningless glitter meant "merely" to convince students to attend the particular college. In addition, if the student is required to adhere to the rules of conduct as if the handbook were a contract, the university has some obligation to adhere to it in the same way. Many judges would not take kindly to a college's effort to escape its obligations by claiming that its apparent promise is not really binding.

At least one state legislature, New York's, has obliged both private and public colleges and universities to formulate specific disciplinary rules and procedures and to register these with state authorities. While courts have held that New York's registration requirement does not elevate the rules of private universities, for legal purposes, to the level of the rules of governmental agents, the fact that the rules are registered with the authorities can aid your contract claim. With its rules filed with the state as a public document, your university cannot reasonably claim that these rules were not a factor in your decision to attend, not known to you when you matriculated, and, thus, not a binding contract.

Private Universities May Not Be "Arbitrary and Capricious"

Many courts agree with the general proposition that disciplinary procedures at private colleges and universities may not be "arbitrary and capricious." This protection flows from ancient common law ideas about how private associations must treat their members. Decent societies have learned to offer certain protections against individuals being subject to the pure whims and arbitrary acts of other individuals. Courts differ, however, on just how dreadful a university's disciplinary process must be before it is unlawful under this principle. Some courts prohibit convictions reached "without any discernable rational basis," and some bar those "made without substantial evidence" or "contrary to substantial evidence." Thus, even when a private college does not promise fairness in its student handbook, other legal doctrines beyond contract law are available to place some limit on just how badly a college may treat a student.

The doctrine prohibiting "arbitrary and capricious" discipline also prevents universities from disciplining students maliciously or dishonestly. A protection from arbitrary punishment is also a protection from discipline meted out with an utterly outrageous or improper purpose.

That's the good news. The sobering news is that no matter how courts in your jurisdiction define "arbitrary and capricious," winning a case based on such a claim turns out to be very difficult in practice. While the courts are very open to detailed reviews of a student's claim that his or her campus's disciplinary procedures are arbitrary and capricious, such claims, in fact, are at present rarely sustained. Courts tend to give very broad respect for the self-government of private associations, including private colleges and universities. Nevertheless, the arbitrary and capricious rule is an important safeguard, because it prevents administrators from establishing truly outrageous disciplinary rules. Without it, there would be nothing to prohibit a private institution from using a flip of a coin to determine a   student's guilt or innocence. Besides, the mere presence of a legal doctrine placing some limit on an institution's power, where that limit is not clearly drawn, often has the effect of restraining the arrogance of power.

Courts indeed will intervene, however, on the very rare occasions when discipline at private universities is without any basis in reason whatsoever. For example, in the case of *Babcock v. New Orleans Baptist Theological Seminary* (1989), the Court of Appeal of Louisiana deter-

mined that a religious seminary had decided, in a manner that was "grossly unfair and arbitrary," not to grant a degree to a student. The court ordered the university to award the student the degree. The student, who had encountered previous disciplinary problems at the seminary, had been allowed to complete his coursework, and had received notice of his impending graduation. Eleven

> **Definitions:**
> **Arbitrary and Capricious**
>
> *Arbitrary: Determined by chance, whim, or impulse, and not by necessity, reason, or principle.*
>
> *Capricious: Characterized by or subject to whim; impulsive and unpredictable.*
>
> --AMERICAN HERITAGE
> DICTIONARY

days before graduation, however, the university decided not to graduate him under a rule allowing it to withhold degrees from those "unfit" to receive them. Further, the student already had secured a court order prohibiting the seminary from punishing him further for his earlier difficulties. The court held that because the university gave no explanation for the sudden unfitness of the student, the discipline was grossly arbitrary and therefore prohibited.

Special State Protections for Speech

Increasingly, students and student groups face discipline not for conduct, but for offensive (and often not so offensive) speech. Private universities, which are not bound by the First Amendment, are generally not prohibited by law in most states from imposing discipline for mere speech, but there are important exceptions.

The United States Constitution does not prohibit private organizations, such as universities, from making rules limiting the speech of those who choose to join them. Some **state** constitutions, however, establish what is known to lawyers as an "affirmative right" to free speech that belongs to every citizen. In states with such provisions, courts have sometimes ruled that there are limits to the blanket rules that private colleges may make restricting speech.

In *State of New Jersey v. Schmid* (1980), for example, the New Jersey Supreme Court ruled that a guarantee in the state constitution—that "every person may freely speak … on all subjects"—barred Princeton University, a private campus, from enforcing too stringent a rule on speech. Princeton had required all persons unconnected with the university to obtain permission before distributing political literature on campus. This case was one of a series decided by various state supreme courts that interpreted the free speech provisions of their respective

state constitutions to give citizens more speech rights than are guaranteed by the First Amendment to the U. S. Constitution. Such decisions have obvious implications to free speech on the campuses of state universities. Some states, however, also have **statutes** that limit the right of private associations—in our case, private colleges and universities—to restrict the free speech of their members. Other states have **civil rights laws** that protect citizens' speech beyond the protection afforded by state or federal constitutional provisions.

If you face charges that relate in any way to speech, you should find out if your **state** constitution or **state** statutes establish such a right to free speech. If your state offers such protections, you may want to defend yourself by going on the offense about your protected speech rights.

You also should check if your state has any laws that insist on the same treatment of private and public campuses in terms of the censorship of speech. California, for example, has a law, the so-called Leonard Law (named after its sponsoring legislator), which gives students at private universities the same speech rights that the First and Fourteenth Amendments guarantee to students at public universities. This statute, passed in 1992, was the basis for a state court's declaration that a code prohibiting "offensive speech" at private Stanford University was illegal.

Sexual Harassment and Sexual Assault Cases

All educational institutions that participate in federal grant and federal aid programs—which includes virtually all private colleges and universities—have special obligations when dealing with complaints of sexual assault or sexual harassment.

Regulations stemming from Title IX of the Education Amendments of 1972—"titles" are sections of laws—mandate that educational institutions receiving federal funding establish "prompt and equitable" grievance procedures to hear and resolve complaints of sexual discrimination. "Discrimination" is now taken to include harassment and assault. This requirement, then, applies to both complaints about systematic discrimination at an institution and complaints against particular persons for sexual harassment and sexual assault. Regulations prohibit colleges and universities from permitting a pervasive atmosphere that creates a "hostile educational environment" on the basis of sex, an atmosphere that inhibits a student's ability to benefit from the educational opportunities and facilities afforded by the college.

Title IX gives victims of sexual discrimination an interest in due process. If a student makes an allegation of sexual assault or harassment, his or her university must pursue the alleged perpetrator in a manner that is "prompt and equitable." If the university does not do so, the student can file a complaint with the Office for Civil

Rights of the Department of Education, which will review the university's handling of the case, and, if it finds that there has been unfair treatment, take corrective action.

While Title IX's guarantee of fair grievance procedures was intended to create a sound system for **victims** of sexual discrimination, such procedures, of course, should also work to the benefit of **persons accused** of sexual harassment or assault, who are, of course, presumed to be innocent until proven otherwise. Indeed, one could argue that the requirement of fair procedures confers rights upon **both** parties in claims of sexual harassment or assault. Some private universities choose not to offer even the most rudimentary safeguards (or even a hearing) to those accused of crimes of violence. Although courts have not yet tested such an argument, it is possible that Title IX would prohibit the expulsion or suspension of individuals accused of sexual misconduct if they had been denied basic fair procedures. The law's mandate of a "prompt and equitable" hearing in order for the **victim** to seek vindication should ensure, in theory, fair treatment for the **accused** as well. An "equitable" procedure, after all, by definition must be a fair one. Students and their defenders would do well to point this out in cases where they are accused of sexual misconduct. How could a process not fair to **all** parties in a case actually be fair?

Some additional protections for students accused of

sexual assault derive from the Campus Security Act of 1990, which requires that educational institutions receiving federal funding create and publish formal rules for cases involving charges of sexual assault. Private universities have no obligation even to have any rules related to most crimes, but under this law they are obliged to codify procedures for dealing with sexual assault.

Due Process at Sectarian Institutions

Some sectarian institutions—seminaries, colleges, or universities that are associated with churches, synagogues, or mosques, for example—have strict rules governing student conduct. Private colleges are allowed to establish and advertise such rules, of course, as long as their regulations do not violate antidiscrimination laws or other statutes. Even then, some religiously required practices that may appear to be discriminatory—above all in areas of sexuality—may be constitutionally protected as "the free exercise of religion." For example, rules mandating the expulsion of homosexual or sexually active students by sectarian institutions are lawful, as are rules dismissing students for lacking "Christian character." In the 1962 case of *Carr v. St. John's University*, for example, the Court of Appeals of New York (the state's highest court) upheld the right of St. John's University, a Catholic university, to dismiss a student couple who married in a civil but not in a religious ceremony.

Although St. John's has since changed its rule that "in conformity with the ideals of Christian … conduct, the University reserves the right to dismiss a student at any time on whatever grounds," such a regulation would still be perfectly lawful. This is because the First Amendment's religious liberty clause, applied to the states by the Fourteenth Amendment, affords considerable autonomy to religious institutions. What may on the surface appear discriminatory might well be simple voluntary adherence to a religious commandment. While not every religious practice enjoys constitutional protection (human sacrifice and the use of sacramental illegal drugs do not, for example), many practices involving adherence to religious doctrine and to the freedom to associate with others of similar beliefs are protected.

If you are considering attendance at a religious institution, you should review its code carefully to see if it satisfies you and if you are willing to be bound by it while there. If you are a member of a religious student group at a secular university, you should be aware of the fact that you have great leeway to associate with those who believe as you do, without being accused of religious discrimination against those with different beliefs.

PART IV: THE ELEMENTS OF DUE PROCESS

Section I: The Charge

Notice

Due process requires that students facing suspension or expulsion from **public** universities for disciplinary reasons be given appropriate notice of the charges against them (in advance of the constitutionally guaranteed opportunity to be heard on those charges). At a minimum, your university must tell you both that a disciplinary action is pending against you and the charge that you face. The description of the charge should state the rule that you are accused of violating, and should describe, at least briefly, the specific act or acts that allegedly violated the rule.

The notice requirement for cases involving possible suspension or expulsion from public universities was established by *Goss v. Lopez*, the landmark United States Supreme Court case on student discipline first discussed in Part II. As the U.S. District Court for the Northern District of New York put it in *Donohue v. Baker* (1997), students, under *Goss*, are entitled to notice that "is reasonably calculated, under the circumstances, to apprise [them] of the pendency of the action and afford them an opportunity to present their objections." That is, students must be informed of the disciplinary action that they face, and they must be permitted to challenge the charges against them.

> **Definition: Notice**
>
> *A formal announcement, notification, or warning.*
>
> --AMERICAN HERITAGE DICTIONARY

The timing and content of such constitutionally required notice varies according to the circumstances. In the case of **less serious misconduct**, notice may be oral and may be given immediately before the informal give-and-take between student and administrator that fulfills the minimal constitutional requirement for a hearing. All that is required in such cases is that students be told of the charges against them before being asked to affirm or deny them. *Goss* also suggests that greater requirements with respect to the timing and substance of notice may be appropriate in cases that are factually complex or that present the possibility of more severe punishment.

While committed to appropriate notice in theory, the courts, in practice, unfortunately find almost all notice appropriate. The courts indeed have found many circumstances where universities failed to live up to *Goss's* requirement of increasingly formal hearings for increasingly serious charges (see Part IV: Section II). They have not dealt similarly, however, with the issue of greater notice. For the courts, notice would have to be extraordinarily inadequate to be viewed as substantially prejudicing a student's case. Thus, while late or scant notification may in fact deny a student the opportunity to mount the best possible defense, the courts basically care about whether or not a student is actually deprived of a meaningful opportunity to be heard. What the due process clause essentially guarantees is a meaningful and fair opportunity to be heard. Nonetheless, the commitment to appropriate notice is there in court decisions, and you certainly should stake a claim to fairness in that regard. The university might be moved by it; one day, a court might be moved by it.

Even in serious cases, though, in terms of current court decisions, notice need only specify the charges against you (your alleged conduct and the rule you allegedly violated). The Fifth Circuit United States

Court of Appeals, in *Dixon v. Alabama State Board of Education* (1961), suggested that if students were not allowed to attend their own disciplinary hearings, then a list of witnesses and of their expected testimony should be given to them. While the United States Supreme Court cited *Dixon* approvingly in *Goss*, courts in practice have declined to apply the witness list requirement to cases where the student **is** allowed to attend the disciplinary hearing. It now seems that the *Dixon* witness-list requirement stemmed more from students' rights to hear the evidence against them, in order to prepare a defense, than from any right to an advance notice of witnesses.

Although your university may be legally required to provide you merely with basic notice a short time before your disciplinary proceeding begins, you surely will want to fight for timely, detailed notice. Sufficient time and reasonable detail about the nature of the evidence against you are crucial to the preparation of an effective defense. Many schools in fact give greater notice than the law requires. If your school's notice does not give you the information or time you need, a simple request, appealing to fairness and common sense, may get it for you. You should be sure to lodge a formal written objection if the university sets a hearing sooner than you are ready to appear. Write a timely and detailed objection that states the reasons why you cannot be prepared in the time allowed. This will preserve your right to claim lack of notice in a campus appeal or in a lawsuit. It might well suffice to persuade the university to give you the kind of notice you need and deserve.

Preliminary Screenings

Fair and decent systems of justice do not go directly from what might be wild accusations to a formal hearing on serious charges. Unfortunately, campus judicial systems are not always fair and decent, and nothing compels them to have some system of screening cases prior to a trial. In the criminal justice system, of course, preliminary screenings in the form of grand jury investigations or what are known as "probable cause" hearings before a judge are generally required before charges are issued. As described in Part II of this guide, however, campus courts are not held to the same strictness as the criminal justice system.

As campuses deal with a larger and larger number of cases where there is no firm evidence from which to conclude guilt, there may be changes in the air. Some colleges and universities already provide for a preliminary investigation, often lengthy, before charges are filed. Also, there are campuses that are increasingly frustrated by irresolvable cases (he said; she said; no further evidence) that never should have gone to hearing in the first place. Thus, while there is apparently no legal right to a preliminary screening before a disciplinary action can be heard, your college or university may have chosen to offer such a screening as part of its own rules. Harvard University drew national attention to due process issues on campus in 2002, when it instituted a procedure to evaluate the merit of allegations of misconduct before beginning formal disciplinary proceedings against students. When a student makes a complaint against another student, for sexual assault or any other disciplinary rule violation, Harvard now requires that the complainant submit a list of possible witnesses or an account of the evidence—**some** measure of **corroborating** evidence—that the disciplinary tribunal might be able to obtain. This effectively operates as a preliminary screening: The college only opens a disciplinary case if these lists of witnesses or these documents suggest that there might be "sufficient corroborating evidence" available to support the charge.

Nonetheless, despite the considerable attention that Harvard's new rule has drawn, due process does not require that campuses conduct a preliminary screening before issuing a complaint and instituting formal disciplinary proceedings against a student. If your campus does not require such a commonsensical practice, it would be a good thing to argue on behalf of such a decent and rational change.

Deferring a Campus Case When There Is a Criminal Prosecution

If you have both a university disciplinary hearing and a criminal trial pending, you will almost always want to get your disciplinary hearing postponed until after the criminal matter is settled. Holding the disciplinary hearing **before** the criminal trial can be very dangerous, because what you say at the campus hearing—where you have far fewer protections than in a court of law—can be used against you in the criminal case. Courts have held, however, that due process does not require campus disciplinary proceedings to be postponed until related criminal matters are settled.

Despite this unfortunate rule, many universities promise students that they will try to postpone campus disciplinary proceedings until the conclusion of related criminal prosecutions. If your university makes this promise, you can usually hold them to it. Note, however, that if you are **convicted** in the criminal case, the university will frequently find you guilty of the student disciplinary charge automatically, on the basis of the criminal conviction. The theory here is that since the standard of proof is so much more stringent in the criminal court, a conviction there means that there was more than sufficient evidence to support the campus charge. On the other hand, **acquittal** in the criminal court does not always mean that the campus tribunal will acquit, since the level of proof needed to convict you on campus is so much less than in a criminal trial. Still, there is considerable advantage to having the criminal trial go first. For one thing, you would have an opportunity to explore fully the evidence against you, since you are guaranteed highly effective due process—that is, procedural and substantive safeguards of your rights as someone presumed innocent—in a criminal court. **If your college insists that you proceed with your campus disciplinary tribunal before your criminal trial is held, it is essential that you get a lawyer**. At the very least, you need legal advice about how to prevent having what you say at the campus tribunal from being unfairly used against you at a subsequent criminal trial. (See Part IV: Section II for a more detailed discussion of this issue.)

Statutes of Limitations

> **Definition: Statute of Limitations**
>
> *A time limit on legal action.*
>
> --AMERICAN HERITAGE DICTIONARY

TARDY CHARGES

Rules that set specific statutes of limitations for campus prosecutions ensure that campus cases will be considered while relevant witnesses are still there at the school. Although the issue has not been widely litigated, universities are almost certainly **not** required to set a statute of limitations for campus disciplinary cases, even though such a statute would ensure that cases are resolved while the evidence is fresh. The amount of due process required in administrative judicial systems is, after all, substantially lower than that required in the criminal justice system. Do not count on common sense to prevail in this matter.

COMPLETION OF ACADEMIC REQUIREMENTS

The fact that you have already completed your graduation requirements but have not yet received your degree does not give you immunity from most schools' disciplinary regulations. Most universities provide that the awarding of a degree is contingent not only on the completion of academic requirements but also on full compliance with the university's regulations throughout your entire career there. The student's time at the university includes the period between the completion of academic requirements and graduation. Where precisely the line is drawn remains unclear. However, when a student at the Johns Hopkins University shot and killed a fellow student in the time between the completion of his academic requirements and graduation exercises in 1996, a court ruled that the university had good cause to dismiss him without a degree. It is best to stay out of even far less serious trouble in the final days before the awarding of your degree.

REVOCATION OF DEGREES FROM ALUMNI

Universities appear to have the authority to revoke degrees from alumni if discoveries are made, after graduation, about the graduates' activities while they were still students. However, because of the extreme nature of revoking a degree, and the possible damages done by such an act, universities must offer a high degree of procedural fairness in such cases.

This unusual issue arises most frequently when universities discover that students who had not in fact completed academic requirements were allowed to graduate as a result of gross error or deliberate fraud. In such cases, courts see the justification for degree revocation in contract law: By the university's contract with the student, the degree was awarded only because of the fulfillment of certain academic requirements. If these requirements were in fact not fulfilled, no degree should have been issued, and the degree can therefore be revoked. While hearings are not usually required in academic cases at public universities (see Part II), they are required in cases where degrees are going to be revoked. This is because taking away a degree already granted is thought to be more serious than deciding not to award a degree in the first place. Contract law also likely binds private universities to offer procedural fairness in degree revocations.

The courts have not yet come to any agreement about

whether degrees may be revoked when universities discover after a student's graduation that he or she committed a serious disciplinary infraction while a student. One case that was litigated concerned a university's claim to have discovered that a recent graduate had embezzled funds from a student club when still a student. In 2000, the U.S. District Court for the Western District of Virginia found no legal problem with the revocation of a degree in such a case. However, in this specific instance, it refused to dismiss the student's lawsuit, because the university might have departed from its disciplinary procedures in hearing his case. The suit was settled before the court had an opportunity to explore the issue further.

One thing, however, is clear in these matters. Although universities may have the right, after affording strong procedural protections, to revoke your degree after graduation for misconduct in your student days, they may not punish you for misconduct that you engaged in after graduation. The university's power has some limits.

Withholding of Degrees or Suspension Pending a Hearing

Universities sometimes suspend students from the moment that charges are brought until the completion of the disciplinary hearing. Some also withhold degrees from seniors who have completed graduation requirements but have pending disciplinary hearings (as when a hearing is postponed until after a criminal trial).

Temporary Suspensions

Temporary suspensions are allowed **only when a student poses an immediate danger to persons or property**. A hearing regarding the temporary suspension must be held as soon as practicable.

The United States Supreme Court explicitly stated in *Goss* that due process allows immediate temporary suspension without a hearing if the student poses an **immediate danger** to people or property. In short, a student accused of a violent assault could be suspended pending a hearing, but a student accused of plagiarism could not. The main purpose of the temporary suspension must be to maintain safety. Although any suspension necessarily has a punitive impact, the primary purpose of a temporary suspension cannot be to punish.

Hearings must be held for such preliminary temporary suspensions. When it is impossible or unreasonably difficult to conduct a preliminary hearing, students may be suspended immediately provided that a temporary suspension hearing is held as soon as possible. When emergency circumstances do not exist, the temporary suspension hearing must be held before the temporary suspension is put into effect. As the amount of due process required varies with the seriousness of the possible sanction, only minimal protections are necessary at temporary suspension hearings. In the case of short preliminary suspensions, your university must give you nothing more than an opportunity to be heard. You can use this opportunity to argue that you do not pose a threat to safety, or that the temporary suspension has a punitive purpose. Universities at such hearings may well be allowed not to consider detailed arguments about why you are innocent, except in cases of obvious error such as mistaken identity. The purpose of such a hearing is to determine if your presence on campus—before your later hearing on the actual charges against you—poses a danger. For longer preliminary suspensions or for longer periods of withholding your degree, the university may be required to meet higher standards of due process.

Substantive Due Process Rights

Distinct from **procedural due process rights**, you enjoy a separate class of rights known as **substantive due process rights** that offer you grounds to challenge vague, overbroad, and unfair rules. In the American understanding of justice, no person may have any of his or her fundamental rights or personal freedoms taken away without both procedural and substantive due process. Public colleges and universities may not improperly or lightly restrict these substantive due process rights by establishing vague or unfair rules.

<table>
<tr><td>

Definition: Substantive Due Process Rights

Substantive due process rights are those that protect a party from unreasonable, excessive, or uncivilized treatment or punishment. Freedom from cruel and unusual punishments and freedom from invasion of privacy are examples of such rights.

</td></tr>
</table>

VAGUE RULES

Substantive due process requires that rules must be written with enough clarity that individuals have fair warning about prohibited conduct and that police and courts have clear standards for enforcing the law without arbitrariness. Without a prohibition of vague rules, life would be a nightmare of uncertainty about what one could or could not do. The courts do not demand mathematical certainty in the formulation of rules, but they can find a law "void for vagueness" if people of common intelligence would have to guess at its meaning or would easily disagree about its application. For example, a rule prohibiting "bad conduct" would surely be declared void for vagueness.

For the courts, the strictness of the requirement of clarity in any particular case depends on the extent to which constitutional rights and values are involved. To punish people for conduct that they could not reasonably be expected to know or guess was prohibited itself raises obvious constitutional concerns, so courts insist that the criminal laws be written with the utmost clarity. Likewise, rules related to First Amendment freedoms must be wholly clear to avoid "chilling" free speech. A rule prohibiting "bad speech," for example, would leave everyone afraid to speak. The courts permit codes that do not directly involve constitutionally protected matters to be written more loosely. For example, ordinary business regulations are not held to the same exacting standard as regulations affecting freedom of the press.

THE FIRST AMENDMENT AND THE "CHILLING EFFECT"

The First Amendment to the United States Constitution provides that "Congress shall make no law… abridging the freedom of speech, or of the press; or the right of the people peaceably to assemble." This rule, that everyone can express himself or herself without undue government interference, is a cornerstone of our liberty and of our democracy.

In free speech cases, the courts have been very careful not to permit any rule that could leave unclear what speech one may or may not utter. If individuals were afraid to speak their minds because of the possibility that their speech may be found to be illegal, the courts have seen, they will likely refrain from speaking at all. Their speech, therefore, would be "chilled," that is, diminished and stifled. Preventing this "chilling effect," so that free people may speak their minds without fear, is one of the essential goals of the First Amendment.

Courts generally have agreed that disciplinary rules at **public** colleges and universities—when those rules do not violate constitutional protections of freedom of speech and freedom of religion—do not have to be painstakingly specific. Disciplinary rules that **might** relate to speech, however, such as rules punishing disorderly protesters, are held to a higher standard, but they still do not need to be as precise as the equivalent rules in the larger society.

If you are charged with violating a vague campus rule, a lawsuit could well defeat the charge if you could show that your conduct might relate to constitutional protections and thus be covered by the rule against vagueness. For example, in the 1969 case of *Soglin v. Kauffman*, the U.S. Court of Appeals for the Seventh Circuit threw out, on grounds of vagueness, the campus conviction of several students for the general crime of "misconduct." The court held that it was unclear whether the students' purposeful blocking of doorways was prohibited under the rule, because the rule "contains no clues which could assist a student, an administrator, or a reviewing judge in determining whether conduct not transgressing statutes is susceptible to punishment."

If your case does not touch on free speech issues, however, you would need evidence of a very striking abuse to get a university rule voided for vagueness. Courts have upheld quite general campus rules in a very wide range of cases. Further, if you did something **obviously** prohibited even by the vague language of the applicable rule, you usually cannot get your conviction struck down merely because there might be questions about whether **other** conduct is prohibited by the rule. Thus, in *Woodis v. Westark* (1998), the U.S. Court of Appeals for the Eight Circuit found that a criminal conviction for falsifying a drug prescription was enough to violate a college rule requiring that students display "good citizenship" and "conduct themselves in an appropriate manner." The rule was admittedly vague, but despite its inadequacies, it was clear enough that the conduct for which the student was convicted in criminal court was covered by it. The more obviously criminal your conduct is at a college or university, the more likely a court will be to rule that it violated even the vaguest of prohibitions.

Private universities are not bound by constitutional prohibitions against vagueness. However, as described in Part III, courts give students the benefit of the doubt in interpreting the handbooks of private universities—because students have no say in writing the rules—and any vagueness is normally resolved in the student's favor. You can use the vagueness of a private university's rules to your advantage in defending against a disciplinary charge, by arguing that your institution did not give you reasonable grounds for expecting that your conduct was prohibited.

OVERBROAD RULES

Laws are said to be **overbroad** if, in addition to whatever else they prohibit, they significantly restrict protected First Amendment freedoms. The doctrine of overbreadth has its roots not in the due process clause, but in the First Amendment's guarantees of freedom of speech, assembly, and press. Often, however, when a provision of a law violates the First Amendment, it is possible to salvage the rest of the law by cutting out the offending section. A law prohibiting physically assaulting and criticizing an official would be successfully challenged, but that would lead to the removal of the ban on criticism, not to the removal of the ban on physical assault. Laws themselves can only be ruled overbroad if they make it impossible to separate their constitutional and unconstitutional provisions without writing a completely new law.

Laws can be vague without being overbroad, but vagueness often contributes to a finding of overbreadth. For example, in *Soglin v. Kauffman* (see above) the U.S. Court of Appeals for the Seventh Circuit found the university's ban on "misconduct" to be not only vague, but also so overbroad as to allow the university to punish any conduct it wished, including conduct protected by the First Amendment. "Misconduct" was found **vague**, of course, because reasonable people obviously could differ easily about what it was, and, thus, about what was and was not prohibited conduct. Campus police and university disciplinary administrators could charge students for doing anything that personally offended the officer or administrator, giving such officials a terribly arbitrary power. "Misconduct" was also found **overbroad**, because the term would stop people from engaging in a wide variety of activities out of fear of doing something improper. The rule would discourage much ordinary daily activity.

Courts have held that university disciplinary standards can be a little more overbroad than standards in the world beyond the campus, just as they can be a little more vague. However, because public universities have less leeway on free speech protections, you may have a stronger case than you might imagine against an overbroad campus rule, because overbreadth does tend to threaten First Amendment freedoms.

UNFAIR RULES

Public universities enjoy broad discretion to set their own rules for their students. Because attendance at public colleges and universities is a privilege extended only to a select group of citizens, institutions may require that their students demonstrate superior moral or ethical standards. Even if courts think a university's rules to be unwise, they do not have the authority to strike them down if these unwise rules nonetheless conceivably relate to legitimate behavioral or academic objectives.

The courts, thus, do give public colleges and universities broad authority to prevent disruptions of the educational process. This, however, most certainly does not give public universities the right to enact rules unrelated to legitimate behavioral or academic objectives. It also does not give them the right to create rules that are arbitrary, that violate the First Amendment, or that intrude unnecessarily upon the rights of privacy or conscience. At a **public** university, you successfully can challenge disciplinary proceedings that are based on an unconstitutional rule.

Public universities are also prohibited from establishing rules that infringe on students' rights of what is known as "personhood," those parts of one's life over which the individuals in a free society are themselves masters. For example, public universities are not allowed to punish students under unnecessarily strict regulations regarding dress and hairstyle. While public **high schools** are allowed to restrict students' personal appearance to some extent in some parts of the country, public **colleges and universities** may make only the narrowest regulations essential to a reasonable and permissible goal. As noted, the law extends more and more rights as students get older. The only regulations of dress and hairstyle that are generally permitted are those required for safety; those requiring professional students—such as medical students interacting with patients—to conform to standards of dress or cleanliness associated with their trade; and those justified by some similarly reasonable and important purpose.

Keep in mind that while private colleges may not make utterly arbitrary rules, they do have the right, as private associations, to abridge even free speech rights and rights of personhood. They are limited by the rules of civilized society, however. They may not commit fraud in attracting students—advertising one thing but delivering another—and they may not violate their contracts, break the law, or offend civilized standards.

FIRE publishes various guides dealing with some of the dreadful violations of substantive rights common to many contemporary colleges and universities. You will need to consult these guides when preparing to defend yourself against disciplinary charges brought on the basis of conduct that is in fact protected by the First Amendment or by substantive due process. Otherwise your plight will fit into the phrase that lawyers often use for a case where a client is given all due process rights but where the result is a conviction (often for a crime or offense that should not be a legal violation): "being due processed to death." Do not let our emphasis on procedural due process in this guide distract you from the substantive defense that you must offer if you are charged with conduct that should not be an offense in the first place.

"CONDUCT UNBECOMING A STUDENT"

Some institutions of higher education have rules that prohibit students from engaging in "misconduct," "dishonorable conduct," or "conduct unbecoming a student." These rules all have potential constitutional weaknesses, and all but the "conduct unbecoming" rule would probably be invalid at public institutions.

As discussed above, a rule prohibiting mere unspecified "misconduct" is almost certainly unconstitutional. Such a rule is utterly vague, offering virtually no useful guidance as to what conduct is prohibited. A rule prohibiting "dishonorable conduct" is less vague, because it specifies the conduct that is not allowed, namely, conduct that lacks honor. Although courts have not explicitly addressed the issue, such a rule is probably unconstitutionally overbroad, because much conduct protected by the First Amendment lacks honor. It is dishonorable to speak meanly to or about your mother, but you have a First Amendment right to be mean in speech (as long as your speech does not cross over into some prohibited realm, by including threats of physical violence, for example).

Rules prohibiting unbecoming conduct are probably valid only when the university has made a statement about the general standards to which students must conform, although, again, the issue has not yet been tested in court. Typically, "conduct unbecoming" rules apply to professions or trades with generally established and understood standards of conduct. The standards of conduct for professionals such as doctors, members of the military, and judges, for example, are so long established, widely known, and generally accepted that these standards of conduct do not need to be spelled out in writing. In contrast, students are not part of a profession or trade with quite as generally accepted responsibilities. Norms of conduct vary widely between different types of universities and areas of the country, and, indeed, the history of student life has been one of constant challenges and changes to such norms. To avoid the problem of vagueness, an institution should express its particular standards for students if it wishes to use a "conduct unbecoming" rule. This can be done in the preface to the student handbook, in a statement of rights and responsibilities, or in some other document. (That way, also, a student could decide if he or she wished to attend such a university.) A "conduct unbecoming" rule that was not accompanied by a fuller description of the university's general expectation for student conduct would probably be nullified by a court.

Automatic Discipline After Criminal Convictions

Courts have not frequently visited the question of whether students can be automatically suspended or expelled from public colleges and universities for criminal convictions. In *Paine v. Regents* (1972), the U.S. District Court for the Western District of Texas held that a University of Texas rule providing for automatic suspension or expulsion of students convicted of drug offenses violated procedural due process. The court based its decision on the fact that the criminal justice system and university discipline systems served different interests. Thus, a hearing must be held to determine whether the interests in public justice that merited a criminal conviction coincided with university interests in protecting the campus community and its educational goals. For example, is it obvious that someone who burned a selective service card or broke the public peace in a demonstration for or against the choice of abortion must be disciplined by a university? Lots of students were convicted in criminal courts for burning draft cards or for disorderly conduct at demonstrations in the 1960s and 1970s. Do today's administrators wish to argue that those students also should have been disciplined by campus tribunals?

Infractions Committed Off Campus

Public universities may discipline students for their conduct off campus, even if the conduct at issue has little to do with university life. Off-campus conduct is considered to be indicative of a student's character, and universities do have a legitimate interest in maintaining student bodies that meet certain standards of character.

Although colleges and universities may discipline students for a wide range of behaviors occurring off campus, some universities have policies that restrict their own disciplinary jurisdiction. Don't get too comfortable, however, if your school's handbook limits discipline to offenses "detrimental to the university" or "adversely affecting the interests of the college." Such phrases can be interpreted to cover off-campus offenses that don't involve other students. Some universities, however, specifically restrict off-campus discipline to offenses that affect other students. If this is the case at your university, you may have a strong claim that the institution may not punish you for your off-campus conduct with regard to nonstudents, because, as noted repeatedly, schools must follow their own rules.

Confidentiality and Judicial Proceedings

Federal privacy laws classify materials about your disciplinary case as educational records. Consequently, your university is obliged by the Family Educational Rights and Privacy Act (FERPA) to keep them confidential (see Part IV: Section III). If your disciplinary matter has not yet reached the police (at which point a great deal of information about it becomes a matter of public record), it is entirely up to you whether to keep it confidential or to tell others—including, if you choose, the media—about it.

Deciding whether to publicize your case during your investigation or hearing is a complex tactical decision. Publicity can have powerful effects on the fate of a charge and on your chances of receiving a fair determination of guilt or innocence. If there is any ambiguity about your guilt, however, you may want to avoid gaining publicity for your case. The heightened scrutiny that media focus brings may draw attention to the deficiencies of your case, and may provoke university officials to institute more severe sanctions because of public pressure or the effects of negative publicity. If the evidence is overwhelmingly or strongly in your favor, however, and if the administration, despite the lack of evidence or the unfairness of a charge, remains stubbornly determined to convict you (because of campus politics, for example), then publicity can often change everything and prevent a false conviction. However, if you are accused of a serious offense, the stigma of being associated with an accusation—even when false—may outweigh the benefits of publicity.

It is a serious matter for universities to release any

information about your disciplinary case to the media without your consent, before, during, or after your hearing. The disciplinary committee is forbidden from revealing your name to the media, and it is similarly prohibited from revealing information easily traceable to you without using your name. In practice, universities tend to be very careful about observing these restrictions.

In the event of a violation of federal privacy laws, you cannot personally sue your university under FERPA, but you can report the problem to the Department of Education's Family Policy Compliance Office. That office can apply a variety of sanctions against the university, including, at the most extreme, revocation of federal funding.

Typically, however, colleges and universities are perfectly happy to obey FERPA's privacy and confidentiality provisions, because universities in general prefer to operate their disciplinary systems outside of the glare of publicity.

Some colleges and universities have rules requiring student defendants to keep confidential the fact that there are disciplinary proceedings against them. Although universities sometimes claim that FERPA requires such rules, it does not. FERPA does not prohibit students from disclosing information from their own records. (As an obvious example, FERPA prevents the university from inappropriately making your grades public. That does not prevent you from talking or complaining about your grades.) However, as previously noted, universities may establish any rules that have a legitimate educational purpose and do not run afoul of constitutional or legal restrictions. Universities may therefore establish rules prohibiting students from publicizing sensitive information about others—even if they establish such rules due to an erroneous belief that they are required to do so by statute.

How to Conduct an Investigation for Your Defense

A thorough investigation is the best way to get the bottom of any complex factual matter. If you are involved in an incident that you think might lead to a complaint against you, it is very much in your interest immediately to gather and preserve any relevant evidence. It is best to be prepared just in case you are charged, especially because charges are so often brought long after the incident, when memories have faded, witnesses have disappeared, and the trail of evidence is cold. You will want to be careful, however, that your manner of gathering evidence does not provoke a formal accusation against you. If you think that the possibility of a formal accusation is particularly remote, it might sometimes be better to let things be.

If a complaint is threatened or brought, you should continue your investigation, or, if you have not already initiated an inquiry, you should begin work immediately. If your investigation involves the interview of witnesses, it may be best to have a lawyer, a trusted professor, or a professional investigator act on your behalf, in order to avoid allegations of what is known as "witness tampering." It is also useful to have your own witness present during an interview, in case the person interviewed later denies that he or she said something. When the interviewee is willing, you will want to tape-record statements or have them written down.

You need to be active and to anticipate the benefits of conducting an investigation on your own behalf. Your goal is to persuade or embarrass the university, by the weight and quality of your evidence, into dropping unfair charges against you or, if it comes to a hearing, into finding you innocent of false charges. The university is your adversary in a disciplinary case against you—however much you might want to think of it as your friend—and there is no guarantee that it will continue to look for evidence that may help you once it has found evidence against you. Sometimes, it is in an administrator's interest to find a scapegoat for ills at the college or university. Further, if you are charged with conduct that is politically incorrect at a liberal university, or with conduct that runs contrary to traditional values at a conservative or sectarian institution, there may be a tendency for the university to overlook evidence in your favor for ideological reasons. Providing the tribunal with a formal submission of evidence in your favor may refocus your case upon the actual facts.

If your investigation discovers facts overlooked by the administration's investigators or the disciplinary committee that you wish to bring to the tribunal's attention, you should submit a statement detailing what the school would have learned had it conducted a more thorough investigation. This is somewhat analogous to what is known as an "offer of proof" in a legal proceeding, which is a statement of what the court would have determined if it had ruled differently on the exclusion of a question or piece of evidence.

University rules may not encourage formal submissions of this sort, or may even attempt to ban them outright, but if you make such a submission, the university will almost certainly read it. It does not want to become known as indifferent to facts and to innocence. Even if the university disciplinary committee refuses to read your submission, you have established a record of both your good faith and the committee's bad faith. Further, you can force the university to include your submission of evidence in the file of your disciplinary case. As discussed in Part IV: Section III, universities must accept and include in a student's file student submissions correcting alleged factual inaccuracies in the file. It is a doubly good idea to make a submission of this sort if you are not able to participate in your disciplinary hearing.

Regardless of the structure of your university's disciplinary process, you should never let an inadequate investigation by the administration hurt your case. If there is something you found that the administration hasn't uncovered, confront them with it. Let them know that your evidence is there and that, if necessary, it will be public knowledge at some point.

Using the Laws About Educational Records to Your Advantage

In preparing your defense, it may be useful to have two types of information that you can obtain under educational records laws.

The Family Educational Rights and Privacy Act (FERPA) of 1974 (see Part IV: Section III) makes students' records confidential. In 1998, however, the Congress amended the law to allow universities to disclose to the public the names of students convicted by campus courts of violent crimes or of sex offenses, along with information about the final results of their disciplinary proceedings. If you are accused of a crime of violence or a sex offense, you should request the data about other campus cases, so that you know how students previously accused of such offenses were treated. This also gives you the ability to contact students who have been in your situation to ask for advice on preparing your case.

In a disciplinary hearing itself, you also may be able to

use a particular part of FERPA to your advantage. FERPA gives you the right to inspect your educational records. Your university must let you inspect all of your educational records—other than police records or hand-written notes—within 45 days of your request. This presumably gives you the right to inspect materials related to your disciplinary case that may be in the college's files. Reviewing these materials would obviously be very helpful, letting you see the details of the university's case against you. This strategy has not yet been tested, but a recent ruling in FERPA law (see Part IV: Section III), makes this a good time for a trial run.

When Student Groups Face Sanctions

Colleges may sanction a student association that collectively engages in activities prohibited by university rules. However, the misdeeds of a few (or even of a majority) of the members of an association do not always justify disciplinary action against the association as a whole. "Guilt by association," absent other evidence, is rightly viewed as a dreadful thing. For such a collective punishment to be just, the group in its totality should have shared a criminal intent or conspired in the commission or cover-up of a crime. This principle should be particularly strong on a public campus where the First Amendment's protection of freedom of association must be honored to some serious degree. The point at which an entire group may be punished for the infractions of a few of its members is, nonetheless, a difficult matter to determine. A prosecuted group should remind the tribunal of the injustice of guilt by association without evidence that the offending members were acting in accord with the organization's practices and policies, with the wishes or knowledge of a substantial number of members, or with the approval of the organization's leadership. The First Amendment's guarantee of freedom of association would mean little if an entire group could be prosecuted, or even disbanded, because of the unauthorized actions of a few.

University authority to punish student groups was acknowledged by the United States Supreme Court in *Healy v. James* (1972). Although the Court offered few clues about exactly what steps must be followed in disciplinary proceedings for student groups, it cited a lower court finding that "fair procedures"—that is, due process—must be honored. Because due process is flexible, exactly what procedures are required depends on the particular circumstances. As a general rule, the constitutional guarantee of freedom of association gives more protection to expressive organizations, such as political clubs, than to social associations such as fraternities.

SECTION II: THE HEARING

The Right to Be Heard and to Hear the Evidence Against You

If you face suspension or expulsion from a public university, you have a legal right to hear the evidence against you and to have an opportunity to rebut it. This right, recall, was first recognized by the United States Supreme Court in *Goss v. Lopez*, where it found the brief suspension of high school students unconstitutional because the students had not been told of the evidence against them and had not been given a chance to respond to it. The Court held that any student facing suspension must be given "an explanation of the evidence the authorities have and a chance to present his side of the story."

The right to be heard, however, does not necessarily extend to a right to a **formal hearing**, that is, a live proceeding at which evidence is taken and witnesses are called. Under *Goss*, public universities may establish any type of proceeding or mechanism that allows accused students a **fair opportunity** to hear the evidence against them and to tell their side of the story fully. Because a fact-finding hearing is the most logical and simple way to fulfill *Goss's* requirements, however, the vast majority of public universities hold hearings in serious disciplinary cases.

In fact, hearings may be required in more serious cases, because *Goss* holds that the more serious the potential sanctions, the more elaborate the requirements of due process. However, the courts have not yet decided with any clarity and uniformity that students actually have a right to a truly formal hearing. Courts do not like to guide the internal proceedings of universities with any great specificity, and they permit university disciplinary proceedings to be much less elaborate than those of criminal trials.

Hearing procedures need not be the same for all offenses. Indeed, the idea that greater protections are needed for increasingly serious charges is a basic principle of due process—even the criminal justice system dispenses with jury trials for minor offenses where the maximum penalty is very modest. Nonetheless, due process also requires that similar cases be handled by similar established procedures. Public universities also are obliged to treat similar cases in a similar way under the Fourteenth Amendment's guarantee of "equal protection of the laws," which requires that the government apply the same rules to people in similar circumstances. Your public university must have a very good reason indeed to handle your case differently from similar past cases.

There are some special cases and situations in which hearings clearly are not required. If you admit your guilt to the charges against you, you waive your right to be heard on the issue of guilt versus innocence. While this may seem obvious, there are cases where students have admitted guilt and then tried to sue their universities for deprivation of due process because they were punished without a hearing. Once guilt is admitted, the reason for a hearing, at least on the issue of guilt, largely disappears. Think about this if your university tries to convince you to plead guilty to a charge of which you know you are innocent. Nonetheless, you might still be entitled to a hearing on the issue of appropriate punishment.

Also, if your university determines that you pose an ongoing threat of disrupting the educational process or an immediate danger of harming persons or property, you may be temporarily suspended without a hearing or notice, provided that a temporary suspension hearing is held as soon as practicable (see Part IV: Section I).

At a private university you do not have a legal right to a hearing—although you certainly should argue for your moral right to one—unless the university promises such a hearing to you and is bound by the principles of contract law in the university's state. Most universities, however, do promise hearings, and if the university says that it will grant you a hearing, you may be able to get the courts to hold them to their word. For example, in *Tedeschi v. Wagner College* (1980), the Court of Appeals of New York ruled that an expelled student who had been granted something less than the actual hearing promised in a student handbook was entitled to reinstatement pending a new and, this time, adequate hearing.

The Right to Hire a Lawyer

A university may not interfere with your right to retain an attorney to assist you in preparing your case. However, public colleges and universities generally may prohibit you from bringing your attorney to your disciplinary hearings. Some courts, however, have recognized a student's right to bring a lawyer to a university disciplinary proceeding if the university's case is presented by a lawyer, or if the violation charged is also being prosecuted—or is likely to be prosecuted—in the criminal courts. Additionally, some states have laws specifically requiring that persons who face administrative proceedings, such as campus disciplinary proceedings, be allowed to retain counsel to represent them. Know your state's laws.

The Sixth Amendment's celebrated guarantee of the right to counsel applies only to criminal trials. In terms of campus disciplinary cases, a claim of right to counsel would have to stem from the due process clause, and most courts have agreed that due process does not require universities to allow students to bring lawyers into ordinary disciplinary proceedings, even when expulsion is at stake. However, since *Goss* does hold that greater due process is required in more serious cases, some courts have taken this to mean that additional procedural protections such as the right to counsel are required in some special circumstances. In *Gabrilowitz v. Newman* (1978), the U.S. Court of Appeals for the First Circuit held that due process requires that students be allowed to retain counsel to advise them at disciplinary hearings when related criminal charges are pending. Because such situations present complicated concerns about self-incrimination, the court held that it would be a denial of due process to force the student to proceed without a lawyer. However, it stated that due process requires only that the lawyer be allowed in the hearing room to advise the student. The college may still ban the lawyer from making arguments and questioning witnesses.

Some courts have also held that when the prosecution's case is presented by a lawyer or another legally experienced person, a university must allow students to retain a lawyer truly to represent them at the hearing, that is, to make arguments and question witnesses on their behalf. In *French v. Bashful* (1969), the U.S. District Court for the Eastern District of Louisiana overturned a disciplinary action against students at a public university because while a third-year law student presented the university's case at the hearing, the students themselves were not allowed to be represented by counsel. It stopped short, however, of ordering the university to provide free counsel for indigent students.

Some states have also established a right to be represented by hired counsel in all state administrative agency proceedings. Because courts sometimes treat public university disciplinary hearings as such administrative proceedings, you may have a right to be represented by private counsel if you go to school in such a state. In that circumstance, a court might well vacate your conviction if you are denied this right. For example, in *Kusnir v. Leach* (1982), the Commonwealth Court of Pennsylvania vacated a student's suspension at a public college because he was not allowed a lawyer, which it ruled a violation of Pennsylvania law establishing a right to counsel in administrative proceedings. Again, it is important to know and use your state law.

Even though private universities may bar lawyers from their disciplinary proceedings, you nonetheless may wish to seek the **advice** of an attorney—even if he or she may not join you at a hearing—unless your case is very minor. In fact, since most of the work on your defense will be done outside the hearing room, a lawyer can provide a great deal of help. You need to weigh the costs involved against the possible harm that you might suffer from an unjust conviction or punishment. It also never hurts to ask whether you may bring your lawyer with you to your hearing. As is the case with many of the other protections we discuss, many universities are more flexible in this area than the law requires.

Composition of the Hearing Panel

A hearing before an **impartial** fact-finder and decision-maker is essential to due process. Indeed, the impartiality of tribunals is one of the hallmarks of a decent society. While the basic principle that the body hearing your case must be free of bias applies to academic disciplinary hearings at **public** college and universities, courts nevertheless have held that certain accommodations may be made to the unique circumstances of institutions of higher education. Administrators may serve on your hearing panel, and panelists may even have had prior involvement with your case. The rules are loose, in other words, but the fundamental principles of fairness and reasonableness still apply.

Hearing boards in university disciplinary cases must be free from unreasonable bias. If you believe that the tribunal that is hearing your case is biased, you should object in writing before the panel even considers your case. Given human nature, you stand the greatest chance of having biased panelists removed **before** the panel has invested time and effort in your case. When you state your reasons for your challenge, you should be as specific as possible, placing facts, not speculations, on the record.

If the panel in your case displayed bias, you will want to raise that as a crucial issue in any formal or informal university appeal process. If all else fails you can file, or threaten to file, a lawsuit on the basis of the panel's bias. To succeed in such a lawsuit you will need to show explicitly that a panelist approached his or her duties after having already formed an opinion regarding the charge. (This is easiest, of course, when a panelist has commented publicly on your case before the hearing.) When this standard of unacceptable conduct is reached, courts will sometimes overturn student convictions. For example, in *Marshall v. Maguire* (1980), a New York court vacated the expulsion of a student at a state university because one individual had served on both his hearing and appeals panels. The court concluded logically that someone who already had voted to convict the defendant at a hearing clearly had formed an opinion on the charge before serving on an appeals panel. In this case, such a denial of due process, which also violated the university's own established procedures, cast a shadow on the university's **entire** disciplinary process, and the court overturned the rulings of both the original and the appellate panels.

In the criminal courts, a defendant may ask for a change in the location of a trial (a change of venue) when too much publicity or a heated atmosphere makes it virtually impossible to secure an impartial jury. Frequently, in campus cases, a defendant faces similar circumstances, but there is no means of changing the location. You face a steep uphill battle if you wish to contend that a general atmosphere on campus denied you an impartial hearing. Even if you show that there was, indeed, an emotionally charged and even poisonous atmosphere against you, you must prove specifically that this atmosphere affected the hearing board's impartiality—a very difficult burden to meet. There have been many cases, however, where a campus atmosphere condemning an alleged offense makes it difficult for students accused of that offense to get a fair hearing. The best thing that you can do if you face a hearing in such circumstances is to tell the board that you share the campus's general sentiment about the heinousness of the crime charged, and remind them of their duty to focus only on the facts of the specific case. Remind them that you are neither a symbol nor a scapegoat, but an individual presumed to be innocent. Point out that there is **no** crime so heinous that **innocence** is an insufficient defense.

Although courts will sometimes overturn your conviction if you demonstrate actual bias, they do permit the presence of panelists who have a prior acquaintance with the matter at hand. In our civil and criminal systems of justice, off campus, judges must disqualify themselves if they have any prior substantial relationship with a matter before the court. However, courts recognize that in the intimate context of the university community, it is inevitable that fact-finders will have some prior acquaintance with the issues on which they are asked to pass judgment. Because few cases challenging the composition of university hearing boards are brought, it is not clear how much prior knowledge is too much. In *Nash v. Auburn University* (1987), the U.S. Court of Appeals for the Eleventh Circuit did not find a hearing board tainted by a panelist's knowing the suspicions against the defendant before serving on the panel. Indeed, the court found it permissible that the panelist had answered questions from some potential witnesses about how to come forward to offer testimony. Rulings in cases such as *Nash* imply, however, that there **is** a level of more substantial previous involvement, as in *Marshall v. Maguire*, that would constitute a denial of impartiality.

In administrative agency proceedings generally, the individual making the decision to prosecute may not be significantly involved in determining guilt or innocence. In *Goss*, however, the United States Supreme Court refused to require separation of the judging and prosecutorial functions in minor high school disciplinary cases and even assumed that for short suspensions at high schools, the two roles would be performed by the same person.

In more serious cases, however, the prosecutor and judge very likely could **not** be the same person, because this would result in a decision-maker with an unacceptable degree of bias and prior acquaintance with the matter. At the very least, you should argue that this is an unacceptable conflict if you are faced by such a situation.

Hearing panels need not be of any minimum size, and even single fact-finders are acceptable. Also, there is no hard-and-fast rule about what percentage of the members of a panel is required in order to convict, although naturally it would have to be at least a majority.

The Victim as Prosecutor

In the nonuniversity criminal justice system, the only role that the victim plays is that of witness. Our system views crime as an offense against society rather than merely against the individual victim, and charges are brought by prosecutors as agents of "the people." At some universities, however, a person reporting a disciplinary offense must personally prosecute the case against the defendant at the disciplinary hearing. Such an arrangement, while legally permissible at both public and private universities, is undesirable. Forcing the victim to undertake the burdensome and painful work of prosecuting cases deters the reporting of crimes and makes conviction dependent not on the merits of the case but on the victim's legal skill.

While a victim probably has no legal right to object to a requirement to be the prosecutor at a university hearing, the accused, at a public university, may have a right to object to such a circumstance. A prosecutor's range of choices—what is known as "prosecutorial discretion"—can have a profound effect on the outcome of a case. Because of that, accused persons, in the nonuniversity context, are entitled to a prosecutor who is impartial before entering the case. Although courts have not considered the question, due process may allow accused students to prevent their accusers from being their prosecutors in the university setting. It may be more effective, however, for either the accuser or the accused, or both, to simply make a nonlegal argument that it is unfair to force the accuser to perform the role of prosecutor.

Proof

BURDEN OF PROOF

The presumption of innocence—"innocent until proven guilty"—is central to both our system and notion of justice. When a public college or university seeks to discipline you, it bears the burden of proving you guilty. Some evidence of your guilt, at least, has to be presented. You then have to be given some opportunity to rebut the evidence.

STANDARD OF PROOF

The standard of proof due process requires in university disciplinary proceedings—that is, the degree of certainty with which a fact must be established for the fact to be determined true—can be a bewildering topic.

Public universities—and, at least in theory, private universities—are required to base their disciplinary decisions on "substantial evidence." This means that, once again in theory, there must be more than some mere morsel of evidence to support a finding of guilt. There should be enough evidence to convince a reasonable and impartial fact-finder of the conclusion.

In fact, however, courts cannot actually hold disciplinary boards to this standard, which is what makes the issue a bit bewildering for those of us who wish that theory and practice coincided in matters of justice. A deep principle of the law holds that when a higher court reviews certain types of decisions made by lower courts, it must defer to the lower court's judgments on certain particular subjects, avoiding second-guessing its findings in these special areas. This is one such area. In order for a reviewing court to throw out the verdict of a university disciplinary hearing on grounds of the standard of proof, it must go beyond finding that the hearing's decision was not based on "substantial evidence." It must find that the verdict was not based on any evidence at all.

If the court finds there was "some evidence" to support the charge, it must, all other things being equal, uphold the ruling. The "some evidence" standard is satisfied if there is any evidence at all supporting the charge, but not if there is no evidence. Most of the time, if the court determines that there was "some evidence," but not what it would consider to be "substantial evidence," it must uphold your conviction. As the U.S. District Court for the Northern District of Illinois court ruled in *McDonald v. University of Illinois* (1974), this somewhat confusing state of affairs is a result of the general principle that reviewing courts should give deference to the decisions of administrative panels.

In cases that involve free speech on public campuses, however, reviewing courts may apply a "substantial evidence" standard rather than one of "some evidence." The reason for this higher standard of review is that there are constitutional implications to these cases.

In theory, private university disciplinary panels also must apply the "substantial evidence" standard of proof to disciplinary decisions. This protection flows from the legal doctrine that private university disciplinary decisions may not be "arbitrary and capricious" (see Part III) and the fact that many courts have ruled that verdicts must be based on "substantial evidence" in order to avoid being arbitrary or capricious. If this doctrine were held to, the right to a decision based on "substantial evidence" would be one of the few procedural protections available to private university students. In practice, however, courts are very reluctant to interfere with the disciplinary decisions of private universities, and they will do so only when such decisions are based on virtually no evidence.

Definitions: Standards of Proof

The following different standards of proof are used by various college and university tribunals. They are defined here in the order of how difficult they are to meet, from the most to the least difficult.

Beyond a reasonable doubt: *"fully satisfied, entirely convinced, satisfied to a moral certainty"*

Clear and convincing evidence: *"reasonable certainty of the truth…the truth of the facts asserted is highly probable"*

Preponderance of evidence: *"more probable than not"*

Substantial evidence: *"such evidence that a reasonable mind might accept as adequate to support a conclusion"*

Some evidence: *any evidence at all supporting the charge*

DIRECT QUOTATIONS ARE FROM BLACK'S LAW DICTIONARY

The standards of proof required of colleges and universities by law, then, are a far cry from those of the criminal justice system, where conviction has to rest on guilt "beyond a reasonable doubt." However, many universities employ a much greater standard of proof than the law requires, and they would be unable to defend morally a lesser criterion. Most use the standard of "clear and convincing" evidence, which requires a reasonable certainty of guilt for conviction. The vast majority of schools employ, at the very least, a "preponderance of evidence" standard, which requires that guilt be more likely than not for conviction. This is a very common-sensical **minimal** standard for proof necessary for conviction. After all, if the "preponderance" guideline is **not** met, this means that most of the evidence argues for innocence rather than guilt. It would be a bizarre system that allowed convictions where innocence was more probable.

In short, you are not likely to win a case against your campus court if your **only** legal claim is that there was some evidence against you, but not enough to establish your guilt with a sufficiently high level of certainty. The court-imposed requirements on issues of standard of proof are very low and very vague. Nonetheless, there are some broad limits to the university's right to convict an individual on little or virtually no evidence, or on the basis of evidence that is overwhelmingly and very reliably contradicted. For example, if someone testified that you committed a crime on campus at a time when you have incontrovertible evidence that you were a thousand miles away, virtually any court would go out of its way to overturn your campus conviction. The victim's testimony that you were the culprit despite that, although constituting "some" evidence, would not very likely satisfy a court's notion of adequacy.

Procedure

FORMAL RULES OF EVIDENCE

What kind of evidence may and may not be used against a defendant in a college or university judicial proceeding? Due process does not force colleges and universities to apply the same rules governing the admissibility of evidence at criminal trials, although many universities in fact employ a few of those rules. In the criminal courts, witnesses may not testify to things that they don't know personally, but about which others have told them. That is called "hearsay," and it is barred from criminal proceedings. By law, however, university disciplinary tribunals may indeed admit hearsay from witnesses as evidence, and most do. In the criminal courts, only sworn testimony is admissible from witnesses. In university tribunals, witnesses do not need to be put under oath. Indeed, at college or university trials, virtually anything may count as evidence. The only requirement is that the rules used allow for basic fairness. If the lack of formal rules of evidence denies you basic fairness, however, then you may have a due process claim.

CROSS-EXAMINATION

On similar grounds of rules essential to basic fairness, you **may** have the right to cross-examine the witnesses against you at a college or university disciplinary hearing, **if such cross-examination is necessary to draw out the truth about the matter at issue.**

The Sixth Amendment guarantees the right to cross-examine witnesses in criminal proceedings. It also gives criminal defendants a right to confront their accusers—that is, to look at them eye to eye when they testify. The Sixth Amendment, however, even as extended by the Fourteenth Amendment, only applies to federal and state criminal proceedings. Whether a right to cross-examination would apply in public college disciplinary hearings would depend upon whether it was essential to the "fair" hearing guaranteed by the due process clause.

Cases where cross-examination is most clearly required are those built solely around factual claims and charges made orally by a witness. For example, in *Donohue v. Baker* (1997), previously discussed, a rape charge against a male student hinged on whether a female had consented to sexual intercourse that both agreed had taken place. The U.S. District Court for the Northern District of New York held that the accused student had the right to cross-examine the alleged victim, because the only evidence that the act had not been consensual was her testimony, and the determination of guilt or innocence therefore rested on her credibility. This case is vitally important, because similar circumstances arise with some frequency. If you are accused of sexual assault, you can use *Donohue*, even if it does not apply directly in your jurisdiction, to argue that basic fairness gives you the right to cross-examine the complainant. Courts in one jurisdiction are very often persuaded by the reasoning of courts in another jurisdiction.

By contrast, however, the U.S. Court of Appeals for the First Circuit, in *Gorman v. University of Rhode Island* (1988), held that you do not have an obvious right to cross-examine witnesses about the more general subject of their potential biases. However, in a case where the defense specifically rests on the bias of witnesses, cross-examination on this topic may well be permitted.

The specific nature and scope of cross-examination required by due process also depend on the circumstances. In *Donohue*, the court found that it was permissible for the tribunal to allow the accused to question witnesses merely by posing his questions to the panel, which then directed them to the witness. Other courts have approved circumstances in which witnesses could refuse to answer a question in cross-examination. The logic of court decisions on this question is that limits on cross-examination that might be appropriate in one circumstance might be inappropriate in others, if it could be shown that such limits denied fundamental fairness to the accused.

Even though the law only requires cross-examination in a limited set of circumstances, many schools allow for cross-examination at disciplinary hearings in a far greater range of circumstances. Once again, if your school **promises** the right of cross-examination in a given situation, it may well be legally obliged to live up to that promise.

Due process, as indicated by *Donohue*, does not generally require face-to-face confrontation in campus disciplinary proceedings. However, if a compelling case could be made that such actual confrontation is necessary to a fair judgment (for example, when someone's defense is based on mistaken identity), it might well be required by due process. As in the case of so many other protections, the extent of the "process that is due" depends largely upon the facts and circumstances of the situation. If you want to argue for more process, you need to demonstrate why such procedural rights are made necessary by the facts and circumstances of your particular case.

CALLING EXCULPATORY WITNESSES

"Exculpatory" evidence is evidence that exculpates you of guilt—that is, that proves or serves to prove your innocence. It is the opposite of "inculpatory," or incriminating, evidence. In *Goss*, the United States Supreme Court did not require that students be permitted to call exculpatory witnesses in cases involving suspension of ten days or less. However, courts have long recognized that students have a right to call witnesses in cases where more serious punishment is at stake. This principle, as applied to universities, originates from the previously discussed *Dixon v. Alabama State Board of Education*

(1961), where the United States Court of Appeals for the Fifth Circuit ordered that an accused student, when expulsion was at issue, must be allowed to "produce either oral testimony or written affidavits of witnesses in his behalf." Although few courts have considered cases where this means of defending oneself was denied, it is fairly clear that in a serious case, due process would be violated if the right to call exculpatory witnesses were not granted.

The right to call witnesses, however, does not appear to extend to a right to compel their attendance at the hearing, although to our knowledge this point has not arisen in a case that **depended** on the attendance of such a witness. If you want the campus tribunal to make extra efforts to force or convince a reluctant witness to appear to testify, you should convince the panelists that the witness is essential rather than merely peripheral to your defense. Again, this differs significantly from criminal trials, where you have a right to compel witnesses to testify in person if their testimony is at all relevant.

THE RIGHT TO BE PRESENT AT A FORMAL HEARING

Under *Goss*, you have the right to hear for yourself an "an explanation of the evidence" against you before you present your defense. As a result, if your public university uses a formal hearing to decide your case, you have the right, even where potential punishments are minimal, to be present at all of the hearing, in order to hear the evidence being used against you. This protection, unlike many of the others we have discussed, applies so broadly because while allowing you to be present creates only a minor burden to the university, it can have a major impact on the fairness of the proceedings.

Courts have overturned convictions in cases where the right to be present at the entirety of a formal hearing was denied. For example, in *Texas Medical School v. Than* (1995), the Supreme Court of Texas overturned the expulsion of a student from a public medical school because the student was not allowed to accompany the hearing officer and a school representative when they visited the site of the alleged offense. Likewise, another court vacated a conviction in a case where new information was given to the hearing board after the conclusion of the hearing and outside of the presence of the accused. This has been an area where obvious doctrines of fairness have generally prevailed.

Open Versus Closed Proceedings

Criminal courts are open to the public in all but the most unusual circumstances. However, under federal laws about educational records, both public and private universities must keep disciplinary hearings closed to the public, **unless the accused student consents to have them open.**

Your right to a closed hearing is guaranteed by the Family Educational Rights and Privacy Act, or FERPA (see Part IV: Section III). FERPA allows universities to share your educational records only with those staff members who have a "legitimate educational interest" in them. This means that you may prevent your university from opening your disciplinary hearing to individuals who have no legitimate purpose in being there. You will not be successful, however, if you object to the presence of staff members whose functions at the university relate to the matter.

As you might expect, administrators tend to opt for closed rather than open proceedings, because it is easier to dispense campus justice (or injustice) outside of the public's critical gaze. You face a tough battle if you want your disciplinary hearing open to the public. At a **private** university you naturally have no right to an open hearing, because private universities can set virtually whatever rules they please, within reason. Courts have generally held that at **public** universities, due process does not require that a disciplinary hearing be open to the public, even if the student requests it. If, however, your college or university claims that it would like to grant your request but is prevented from doing so by FERPA, you will prevail. FERPA gives the accused the right to a closed hearing; it does not prevent the accused from having an open one. You also may find it effective to make at least the moral argument that your hearing should be open to the public, asking your college or university what it has to hide.

Presumptions From Silence

Unlike the circumstances of a criminal trial, the disciplinary hearings of a public university do not give you the right to refuse to testify. Indeed, your silence at such a campus hearing can be used against you.

The Fifth Amendment guarantees that no person shall be compelled to incriminate himself in a criminal proceeding. It reflects a deep respect for the sanctity of a person's innermost being. As a result, accused persons may refuse to answer questions put to them in criminal proceedings—the celebrated "right to remain silent." In criminal law, no inferences whatsoever, negative or positive, may be drawn from the silence of a criminal defendant.

While defendants have a right to remain silent in criminal court, students do **not** enjoy such a right at college disciplinary hearings, although a few universities do voluntarily provide this right. Your university may compel you to give testimony that may hurt you in any number of ways, and it may punish you for refusing to testify.

However, if you make self-incriminatory statements under compulsion in a public university disciplinary hearing—that is, if you are forced to make statements against your will because of severe penalties for silence—

it is possible that these statements may not be used against you in criminal court. In 1967, the United States Supreme Court established a general rule, in the case of *Garrity v. New Jersey*, against the introduction in criminal proceedings of compelled statements from administrative hearings. This precedent has been applied to universities in cases such as *Furutani v. Ewigleben*, decided by the U.S. District Court for the Northern District of California in 1969.

More commonly, universities do not establish special and specific penalties for silence but state, instead, that a failure to testify will be weighed against the student. This is legally acceptable to the courts. The United States Supreme Court, in *Baxter v. Palmigiano* (1976), ruled that interpreting silence negatively is acceptable in administrative hearings if the use of the privilege not to testify is not directly punished. This ruling was applied to university disciplinary hearings in the case of *Morale v. Grigel* (1976).

Unfortunately, testimony given under a threat that harmful inferences will be drawn from silence, rather than under a threat of direct penalties, is usually admissible in a criminal trial. In *Gabrilowitz v. Newman* (1978), the United States Court of Appeals for the First Circuit ruled that such testimony was voluntary, not compelled in any unconstitutional sense.

In choosing whether or not to make a statement at your disciplinary hearing, you should generally give the highest priority to protecting your interests in a potential criminal case. After all, the consequences of a criminal conviction are in almost all cases much graver than those imposed by a university. It is almost always a good strategy, therefore, to do everything possible to have your disciplinary hearing postponed until **after** the conclusion of your criminal case (see Section IV: Part I). If you are unable to do this, you should never assume that if you testify at the disciplinary proceeding, damaging statements will be inadmissible at a later criminal trial. Consult a lawyer fully familiar with the law in your jurisdiction if you truly need to know whether or not your campus testimony would be admissible in the criminal case. There is a common understanding among most attorneys and people of common sense: If you have something to hide, **for whatever reason**, it is almost always better to remain silent. Even if your university states that it will draw negative inferences from your silence, it is better to say nothing if what you say could potentially be incriminating in a criminal court.

It is painfully easy to suffer from failing to follow this important and reasonable advice. For example, some students have been charged and convicted in criminal court on the basis of a mere apology given in the context of a campus proceeding. An accused student is sometimes told by a campus advisor that the tribunal might go easier on him if he apologizes, and then this apology is deemed evidence, in a criminal court, of his guilt. When the misconduct with which you are charged on campus is also a violation of the criminal law, proceed with the greatest caution, and only upon the advice of an experienced, skilled criminal defense lawyer.

Tape Recording and Transcript of Proceedings

In the majority of cases, courts have held that due process does not require the college or university holding a hearing to make transcripts or recordings of the proceedings. (To say the least, the absence of a record makes both appeals and suits against the university for wrongful actions far more difficult.). To our knowledge, no test case has arisen in which a student has alleged a due process violation because the right to record a hearing has been denied. However, if a university, public or private, has a rule requiring or permitting a recording or transcript, then that promise generally is enforceable.

This area has not been frequently litigated, and courts have not given extensive explanations of their decisions in such matters. Remarkably, the courts appear to believe that the burden imposed on the university by requiring it to record a hearing outweighs the potential harm done to the student from the absence of such a record. Some courts, however, have held that universities must allow students to make recordings of disciplinary hearings at the students' own expense. The reasoning here is that this obviously does not impose any cost on the university.

Nonetheless, many universities forbid the recording of disciplinary proceedings by anyone. If your university has a ban and you in fact wish a record, you should challenge the rule as being without any reasonable basis or purpose.

Complainants With a History of Lodging False Accusations

In the nonuniversity criminal justice system, the names of alleged crime victims typically become a matter of public record when a criminal case is brought. However, under educational records privacy laws (see Part IV: Section III), universities are obliged to keep confidential the names of persons who make accusations of misconduct. While the secrecy of the university disciplinary process has certain valuable aspects, it removes the great protection against false or malicious accusations that the open nature of the criminal justice system provides. You have no way of knowing whether the person accusing you has made false accusations against other students on other or even many occasions.

While the university itself is prohibited from informing you that your accuser has a history of lodging similar and demonstrably false accusations, the prior victims of this false accuser are not barred by law from speaking. If you can find these individuals, they may be willing to testify on your behalf or otherwise help you. In a serious case, where you suspect you are being falsely accused by a person with a history of making false accusations, your lawyer may want to hire a professional investigator to examine whether this is the case. If you believe that publicity will not otherwise hurt your case, you may want to make your plight public in order to prompt others who have suffered at the hands of the same accuser to contact you. You might run into difficulty, however, if the university warns you to protect the privacy of your accuser and not to disclose his or her name (see Part IV: Section I). If your university has such a requirement, and you believe that it is hurting your case, you should make a detailed written presentation to the disciplinary tribunal explaining precisely why your defense will be hampered by your inability to conduct an investigation that uses the name of your accuser.

Similarly, if your accuser's name is secret, witnesses to whom the accuser may have made statements that could prove your innocence are less likely to come to light. Gathering evidence in a secret case is always more difficult than doing so in a well-publicized public proceeding.

Acquaintance Rape and Consent

Rape is the most serious crime that frequently comes before campus courts. The great majority of campus rape cases, however, do not involve violent stranger rape.

CHARGES THAT THREATEN FREE SPEECH

The due process to which you are entitled in a university disciplinary hearing, we see clearly by now, varies by the circumstances of your case. Because First Amendment rights are so sacred, courts often hold that a greater amount of process is due in cases that involve freedom of speech, assembly, and the press. For example, standards of proof must be higher in speech cases, and rules and regulations must be more clear and specific. If your case has First Amendment implications, it is always a good idea to highlight these in order to support your argument for a higher level of due process. Even from a strictly tactical perspective, when you are able to defend yourself on free speech grounds, you almost always find yourself fighting from higher moral ground than would otherwise be the case. Students defending themselves in cases that involve free speech should consult FIRE's *Guide to Free Speech on Campus*.

Most are charges of what is known as "acquaintance rape," or "date rape," where a sexual encounter took place between people previously known to each other, but where one claims afterwards that he or she did not give consent.

Date rape is a painful reality on campuses, as else-where in our society. Each offense is an extremely grave matter. If you are the victim of an acquaintance rape on campus, however, you usually have resources open to you that are not generally available off campus. Further, the relative confidentiality of the university disciplinary process guaranteed by federal student records laws makes it easier for you to come forward without your name and accusation immediately becoming a matter of public record, as is sometimes the case in the criminal justice system. The recognition of the incidence of date rape is also greater on campus than off campus, so most colleges also have extensive, free counseling resources that can at least help you to come to terms with what has taken place.

The accessibility of the disciplinary process, and the attention given to date rape on college campuses, how-ever, can have serious negative consequences for the accused (whose innocence always should be presumed). On campus, accusations of date rape might be lodged in cases where there is, at best, ambiguity about whether consent was granted, and, at worst, where consent was quite clearly granted but where a campus prosecution goes forward anyway. Unfortunately, some campus judicial systems employ procedures that are so deficient that they cannot discriminate between meritorious accusations and accusations completely lacking in merit.

College disciplinary procedures are not designed to handle cases involving the subtle and complex issues typically involved in date rape cases. For example, the "substantial evidence" standard of proof, while adequate in simple cases, fails in many date rape cases. In a pure "he-said, she-said" case, accusation alone could be judged as sufficient to meet the burden, since what the alleged victim said might be judged by itself to satisfy such a standard. The heinousness of real rape can also overwhelm campus judicial systems and cause convictions in cases lacking merit, especially where well-meaning campus activists constantly draw attention to the alleged prevalence of date rape. Moreover, mere accusation in the campus disciplinary proceedings is usually sufficient to lead to a full hearing; there is usually no preliminary screening step to protect students from being hauled into a tribunal on the basis of misguided or wholly inadequate accusations.

Unfortunately, there is no magic formula for approaching acquaintance rape allegations. If accused of date rape, you should hire an attorney and argue for the fair hearing to which you are entitled by due process. At a public university, highlighting the gravity of the charges may help get you greater procedural protections, as more serious charges require greater due process. At a private university, this is also a powerful moral argument. In a civilized society, the more serious the charge, the greater the protections that are offered to a defendant.

If you are falsely accused of date rape in campus courts, the good news is that a parallel criminal action is far from inevitable. The confidential and highly accessible university disciplinary process invites accusations that rightly would not survive, and, in fact, would never be made in the highly public criminal justice system. Furthermore, when date rape charges are reported to the criminal courts, prosecutors often choose not to bring the cases, recognizing when guilt cannot be established beyond a reasonable doubt. (It is one of the sad aspects of acquaintance rape cases, of course, that just as it is easy for the innocent to be convicted, it is also easy for the guilty to go free.)

Ironically, however, it is sometimes advantageous for the accused in a campus disciplinary matter if campus date rape accusations are accompanied by parallel charges in the criminal court. In such a situation, it may be possible to convince your college to postpone campus proceedings until the criminal trial has occurred. In a real court, you have rights to fair process and reasonable safeguards that are far more rigorous than even the best campuses offer. Your trial may bring to light exculpatory evidence and may produce a favorable verdict that you would not likely achieve if the campus case were tried first. If you are acquitted in a criminal trial, that verdict, in addition to the exculpatory evidence gathered at the trial, can prove very useful in winning your case in the campus tribunal.

Since the prosecution's burden of proof at a criminal trial is "proof beyond a reasonable doubt," campus prosecutors sometimes claim that acquittal in a court of law should not automatically require acquittal in the campus tribunal, where the level of proof needed for conviction is much lower. An acquittal in the criminal courts, however, can make successful campus prosecutions considerably more difficult, because universities may be reluctant to make factual findings that are different from those of other, more rigorous bodies that have considered the same case. Although your first and absolute priority if accused of date rape should always be avoiding criminal exposure, being charged in the criminal court can lead to a favorable campus outcome that you might not be able to obtain otherwise.

SECTION III: CONVICTION AND PUNISHMENT

Notice of Decision

Due process requires that you be informed promptly of the disciplinary board's decision in your case once it has been rendered.

In considering your case, however, the disciplinary panel does not need to come to a verdict. Campus due process permits the panel to decide, in the absence of evidence of your guilt, not to render any verdict at all, or to postpone the proceedings indefinitely until new evidence becomes available. This differs considerably from the criminal justice system, where, once accused, a defendant is entitled to a speedy trial and verdict.

Privacy laws bar universities from revealing the disposition of a disciplinary matter to complainants, except in the case of accusations involving violence or sex (see "Privacy of Records," below).

Written Findings

Courts disagree on whether due process requires written findings in student disciplinary cases.

Many courts have ruled that due process entitles students to at least brief written rulings that state the disciplinary committee's decision. Some courts have gone further and held that due process requires that such rulings state both the specific rationale for the decision and the factual findings behind it. We know of no case, however, where the lack of written rulings was seen as so outrageous an error that the disciplinary board's findings were overturned. This does not mean that no such case exists, but clearly this is not a common ground for judicially attacking a disciplinary outcome.

Many colleges and universities provide for written findings even where the law does not require them. If your school does not automatically provide written findings, it is a good idea to request them nonetheless. They can be critical to your preparation of an appeal or legal challenge.

If your university has issued written findings in your case, and you believe that they contain lapses in logic, you can use these findings in a lawsuit alleging violation of due process, of the university's rules, or of state rules for administrative hearing boards. Courts indeed have overruled disciplinary decisions on such grounds. In *Hardison v. Florida A&M University* (1998), for example, the Court of Appeal of Florida reversed a disciplinary panel's finding on the basis of the written findings. The university had convicted the student for assault and battery, but the court found that the facts reported in the written decision were insufficient to meet the university's own definition of assault and battery.

Appeal

The law does not require public universities to provide an internal avenue for appeal of student disciplinary decisions. Students have a constitutional right only to a single, reasonably fair internal hearing.

The great majority of universities, however, rightly allow an appeal. Further, irregularities in the appeal process may be grounds for a contract claim against your university. For example, in the case of *Mitchell v. MacGuire* (see Part IV: Section III), a New York state court overturned both a student's original conviction and the appellate decision upholding it because of irregularities in the appeals process. Be aware, however, that an appeal sometimes can result in an **increase** in the severity of punishment. Before you decide to appeal an adverse verdict and punishment, check your college's handbook to see whether an appeal permits such an increase in penalties. If it does, then you need to weigh carefully the risks and rewards of pursuing an appeal.

A meaningful appeal is an extremely important procedural protection, because it helps to ensure that all other procedural protections to which you are entitled actually were given to you. If the body initially hearing your case knows that you have a right to appeal, it is more likely to treat your case properly, to avoid the embarrassment of its decision being reversed. When you argue for greater procedural protections at your initial hearing, you should make clear that you plan to appeal if you are not granted the safeguards that you believe you need for a fair trial.

Even if your university doesn't allow a formal appeal process, you should not be deterred from writing to administrators to ask for reconsideration. You can write first to the supervisors of the disciplinary process or to the dean of students, and, if this fails, to the provost, president, and board of trustees. Always write as if these higher officials obviously would care about justice, fairness, and the truth of a case.

Writing Letters of Complaint to University Officials

Many universities tell a students involved in campus cases that the disciplinary process being "confidential," defendants may not discuss the cases with anyone other than advisors, attorneys, or family members. Such policies have the effect, and too often the intention, of prohibiting students who are being mistreated from bringing their cases to the attention of the media and the university community. Nothing in federal law, of course, prevents you from discussing your own case.

The administrators in charge of the disciplinary process would be hard pressed, however, to accuse you of violating the university's confidentiality policy if you spoke about the abuses in disciplinary procedures with their superiors, namely the provost, the president, and even the trustees of your university. Because the duties of these officials include supervising the disciplinary process, it is difficult to argue that it would be a breach of confidentiality to write to them. It is even probable that a public university student is entirely within his or her rights to bring unfair treatment to the attention of political figures such as legislators or the governor, on the theory that they are the ultimate heads of a public university system. (The First Amendment, recall, actually has a provision guaranteeing a citizen the right to "petition the government for a redress of grievances.")

If you find yourself in great difficulty, and facing abuses of power, you may want to write to one or more of these officials, all of whom might well be able to help your case. These officials may notice injustices that lower-level administrators simply ignore. Your very act of complaining to a top university official might produce more meaningful review, because lower-level administrators will be in the unaccustomed position of having their superiors looking over their shoulders. Administrators often take pains to hide abuses from the attention of trustees. Complaining to trustees is a tactic that is too rarely used by aggrieved students. Sunlight, as Justice Louis Brandeis accurately said, is the best disinfectant.

Penalties

Universities enjoy wide discretion in establishing the punishments that they choose for particular infractions. Courts normally will defer to the judgments of university officials on matters of punishment, even if they think that the punishments are unwise, unfair, or excessive.

Nonetheless, the punishments that the university gives to students may not be drastically disproportionate to the offenses of which those students have been convicted. As one court put it in the high school context: "A school board could not constitutionally expel forever a pupil who had committed no offense other than being five minutes tardy one time." A sentence that is wildly out of proportion to the violation committed may cause a court to find a violation of substantive due process. Courts do not like to fine-tune a university's judicial system, but they often will react very negatively to unreasonable punitive extremes.

Student defendants often ask whether public universities may punish them by removing them from extracurricular activities such as sports or by suspending them from aspects of campus life such as on-campus housing. These sanctions are permissible. Universities may also punish students by asking them to attend courses or workshops designed to help them avoid misconduct, such as meetings for alcoholics or anger management classes. It is probably unlawful, however, for **public** universities to **force** you to attend programs whose goal is your adoption of **officially sanctioned views on controversial topics** such as race, sex, or sexual orientation, even if your offenses relate to your views on these subjects. (See FIRE's *Guide to First-Year Orientation and to Thought Reform on Campus.*)

Fines are also acceptable as punishments, as long as they are not so excessive as to put a grossly unequal burden on rich and poor students. In the latter case, a campus appeal might successfully be pursued on grounds of economic discrimination and disparate treatment on the basis of economic status. Such grounds would not likely succeed in court as a due process claim, but might have substantial moral force in a campus appeal.

Privacy of Records

Federal law requires all colleges and universities—public and private—to keep the records of student disciplinary cases confidential, but to disclose these records to the defendants upon their request.

The Family Educational Rights and Privacy Act (FERPA) of 1974 makes a student's "educational records" confidential, but it gives students and their parents the right to inspect them. FERPA is quite specific in delineating precisely who may and may not see a student's records and under what circumstances. Your rights under FERPA are much clearer than your due process rights, which come from judicial precedent rather than statute and which vary widely by both specific case and jurisdiction. Furthermore, unlike due process, FERPA applies equally to all institutions, public or private, that receive any Department of Education funding—that is to say, virtually all colleges and universities.

For some time, there was ambiguity over the extent to which FERPA applied to disciplinary records. However, a number of recent cases, including the extremely important 2002 ruling of the U.S. Court of Appeals for the Sixth Circuit in *U.S. v. Miami University*, now make it wholly clear that disciplinary records are "educational records" and are consequently covered by FERPA.

FERPA therefore gives you the right to inspect any and all documents about you created by the university in the course of your disciplinary case. Others may not examine those records. As with your transcript, the substance of your disciplinary file is confidential. The university may not share information in it, even orally, with anyone other than you and certain specific university officers and staff, unless you waive your rights to such confidentiality.

You have the right to see not only material that has been placed in your official file, but all documents about your case created by the university, no matter who created them or where they are stored. You don't have a right to see notes, however, such as the handwritten notes at meetings that individual administrators or professors made for their personal use and that they have not shared with others. There is no way under FERPA to access a school official's personal notes unless the official gives them to you voluntarily. (It never hurts to ask, however.) Additionally, you don't have a right to see records generated by the campus police that were not turned over to the disciplinary committee. These are considered regular police records. The police may show them to other law enforcement agencies, or to prosecutors, all subject to their normal rules. You can try to see these records under state freedom of information laws, but this is very difficult or even impossible in many jurisdictions.

ACCESS TO RECORDS

If you wish to inspect the records of your disciplinary case, your college or university must gather them and give you access them to them within forty-five days. (See Part IV: Section I, on how you can use this right to your advantage in preparing your defense.) Your university is not required to let you photocopy these records, and many universities do not allow students to copy them. Universities are required to allow you to copy them, however, if preventing you from doing so effectively prohibits you from seeing them.

At the conclusion of your case, if your university has decided to permanently retain documents about you that you would rather see destroyed, you may ask the university to discard them. If administrators refuse to do so, you have the right to a hearing before an impartial officer of the university to ask that the materials be removed. If you can demonstrate at that hearing that the information in your file is inaccurate, misleading, or otherwise in violation of your privacy rights, the university must correct your records. The law specifically allows the university to maintain records about disciplinary actions taken against you, however, so it is unlikely that you will succeed in having your disciplinary record expunged at such a hearing. However, FERPA requires that you be allowed to place a statement in your file explaining any problems you see with any aspects of your educational records, which the university must release if, under circumstances such as a court order, it releases the records themselves.

Your college or university has the right to disclose information about your disciplinary case to your professors or university officials **if they have a "legitimate educational interest" in them**. When you apply to graduate or professional school, or seek to transfer schools, your college may forward any records related to you, including information about your disciplinary record. In such a case, however, it must inform you that this is its policy or make a reasonable attempt to contact you with regard to the transmission of the records.

RELEASE OF RECORDS

If you are found responsible for **certain types of misconduct**, the Higher Education Amendments of 1998 give your university the right to report your name and the final result of your case to specific categories of people.

If you are found responsible for a crime of violence or a sex offense, your university **may** disclose your name, the violation you committed, and the punishment you received to any member of the public, including the news media. Universities do **not** have an **obligation** under FERPA to reveal this information. They may refuse requests to divulge it. Even if your university chooses to speak to the press, however, it may disclose only the final result of your case, keeping the documents related to it confidential. You should note, though, that under the Clery Act of 1990, universities are **required** to make reports to the general campus community about certain very serious crimes that are reported to campus security or the local police. (See the next section for more on when universities must report crimes to the police.) The content of these reports, however, may not be such that it will violate your rights under FERPA.

If you are charged with an act of violence, your college or university **may** tell the victim whether or not you were found responsible. If you are charged with a sex offense, the university **must** tell the victim whether or not you were found responsible. The university is **not allowed** to tell the victim about the outcome of cases involving any violations or rules beyond these categories, such as nonviolent theft.

Whether a school may tell your parents about your disciplinary case depends on the nature of the accusation, whether your parents claim you as a dependent on their tax return, and, for some types of accusations, your age. If your parents declare you as a dependent on their tax return, your school may show them all of your educational records, including your disciplinary file. Most parents declare their college-age children as dependents on their tax return, so if you are a college student your parents likely have access to your disciplinary file. Whether or not your parents claim you as a dependent, a university may tell your parents if you are found responsible for an offense involving drugs or alcohol, if you are under twenty-one at the time of disclosure. Also, as noted above, the university may tell anyone it pleases—including your parents—if you are found responsible for a violation of disciplinary rules involving violence or sex. Within the boundaries of the law, however, universities may set their own policies about when to divulge disciplinary records to students' parents. Under no circumstances, however, is a college or university **required** to tell a student's parents of the student's record. Except in the circumstances mentioned above, your university has an affirmative obligation not to tell your parents about the final result of your case. Thus, if you are not a dependent and are found responsible for nonviolent theft, for example, your university may not reveal this information to your parents.

Universities take their obligations under FERPA very seriously. Although, as noted, you may not directly sue your university for improperly disclosing your records, you may file a complaint with the Department of Education's Family Policy Compliance Office (www.ed.gov/offices/OM/fpco/) if you believe that your university has acted improperly on a FERPA issue. The Department of Education can cut off federal funding from universities that have a practice or policy of violating FERPA.

THE VICTIM'S RIGHT TO CONFIDENTIALITY

Colleges and universities may not reveal the names of witnesses or crime victims without their consent. However, if your university creates records about the allegations that you made or crimes that you witnessed, your parents may see them if your university grants them the right to review your file. A university may let your parents see your file only if you are declared a dependent on your parents' most recent tax return. If a notation that you were the victim of or witness to a crime is placed in your permanent file and you do not wish it to be there, you have the right to ask your university to remove it and,

Typically, however, individual violations of FERPA do not tend to result in significant sanctions.

Reporting of Crimes to Police and Prosecutors

If at any time your university suspects that you have violated the law, it can tell the campus police. Though the rules are not entirely clear, universities might be allowed to forward substantive information in your disciplinary file or perhaps even actual disciplinary records to the campus police. However, the university administration may not, absent a health or safety emergency, disclose confidential information from your school records to

if the school refuses, you have a right to a hearing before an impartial officer of the university. The hearing officer has the power to order that your records be modified if they are inaccurate, misleading or otherwise in violation of your privacy rights.

Universities may send reports containing the names of witnesses or crime victims to the police or prosecutors under certain circumstances. At this point, the fact that you were the victim of or witness to a crime may become available under public records laws, and may be accessible to your parents and the larger public.

non-campus law enforcement agencies (such as local or state police) or to prosecutors. Though the campus police cannot disclose confidential student record information that they have received from university administrators to other law enforcement agencies, they may report the results of their own investigation to non-campus law enforcement organizations or to prosecutors.

If you are found responsible for a crime of violence or a sex offense in a campus disciplinary proceeding, the university may at that time choose to report your name and the fact of the finding of responsibility to non-campus police or prosecutors. The university does not need to inform you when it has done so, but must make a notation in your file that the records have been disclosed. Unless your case is in juvenile court, however, the university may not disclose any information about the case (other than your name, the accusation, and the final result) without a subpoena—that is, without a formal, written and (usually) court-authorized order. Nonetheless, it is relatively easy for police, grand juries, or—in some jurisdictions—attorneys seeking monetary damages in civil suits to obtain a subpoena for all of the university's records related to your case. The university is required to make a reasonable effort to inform you that it received a subpoena of your records before complying with it, unless the subpoena requires the university not to give such notice. Individuals can be subpoenaed as well: if university officials are subpoenaed and asked questions about your records, they must answer.

When very serious crimes have been reported to the local police or campus security, the university has a responsibility to warn the campus community that such crimes have occurred under the Clery Act of 1990 (see previous section).

CONCLUSION

Forewarned is forearmed. Despite certain rights of privacy, you enjoy far fewer protections and safeguards on campus than off campus if you are accused of wrongdoing. There are limits, however, to the arbitrary authority of college and university administrators over you, especially at public colleges and universities, but also at private ones. This guide has sought to inform you of your legal rights. It has sought throughout to clarify the moral arguments on behalf of the procedural and substantive safeguards that should be given to the individuals of a free and decent society. It has explained to you the means at your disposal to defend yourself, your honor, and your rights. If you have to use this guide, we hope fervently that it increases the justice and fairness with which you are treated, and that it aids you in establishing the truth. We also hope that many readers have no need of this guide to protect themselves. If you are in that fortunate category, please use this guide to make your campus one that offers the civilized procedures and protections that you would wish for yourself, your friends, and your loved ones. Justice is an immeasurably precious thing, and due process is an essential part of justice.

APPENDIX: THE FIRST, FIFTH, AND FOURTEENTH AMENDMENTS

Amendment I

Congress shall make no law respecting an establishment of religion, or prohibiting the free exercise thereof; or abridging the freedom of speech, or of the press, or the right of the people peaceably to assemble, and to petition the government for a redress of grievances.

Amendment V

No person shall be held to answer for a capital, or otherwise infamous crime, unless on a presentment or indictment of a grand jury, except in cases arising in the land or naval forces, or in the militia, when in actual service in time of war or public danger; nor shall any person be subject for the same offence to be twice put in jeopardy of life or limb; nor shall be compelled in any criminal case to be a witness against himself, nor be deprived of life, liberty, or property, without due process of law; nor shall private property be taken for public use without just compensation.

Amendment XIV

Section 1. All persons born or naturalized in the United States and subject to the jurisdiction thereof, are citizens of the United States and of the state wherein they reside. No state shall make or enforce any law which shall abridge the privileges or immunities of citizens of the United States; nor shall any state deprive any person of life, liberty, or property, without due process of law; nor deny to any person within its jurisdiction the equal protection of the laws.

CASE APPENDIX

The following cases were each discussed in the text of the guide. Their precise legal citations are below. The cases are listed in their order of appearance.

Mathews v. Eldridge, 424 U.S. 319 (1976).

Goss v. Lopez, 419 U.S. 565 (1975).

Board of Curators of the University of Missouri v. Horowitz, 435 U.S. 78 (1978).

Ewing v. University of Michigan, 474 U.S. 214 (1985).

Vaksman v. Alcorn, 877 S.W.2d 390, 397 (1994).

Morrison v. University of Oregon Health Science Center, 68 Ore. App. 870 (1984).

Giles v. Howard University, 428 F. Supp. 603 (1977).

Schaer v. Brandeis, 432 Mass. 474 (2000).

Fellheimer v. Middlebury College, 869 F. Supp. 238 (1994).

Babcock v. New Orleans Baptist Theological Seminary, 554 So. 2d 90 (1989).

State of New Jersey v. Schmid, 84 N.J. 535 (1980).

Carr v. St. John's University, 12 N.Y.2d 802 (1962).

Donohue v. Baker, 976 F. Supp. 136 (1997).

Dixon v. Alabama State Board of Education, 294 F.2d 150 (5th Cir. 1961).

Soglin v. Kauffman, 418 F.2d 163 (1969).

Woodis v. Westark, 160 F.3d 435 (1998).

Paine v. Regents, 355 F. Supp. 199 (1972). Affirmed by 474 F.2d 1397.

Healy v. James, 408 U.S. 169 (1972).

Tedeschi v. Wagner College, 404 N.E.2d 1302 (N.Y. 1980).

Gabrilowitz v. Newman, 582 F.2d 100 (1978).

French v. Bashful, 303 F. Supp. 1333 (1969).

Kusnir v. Leach, 64 Pa. Commw. 65 (1982).

Marshall v. Maguire, 102 Misc. 2d 697 (1980).

Nash v. Auburn University, 812 F.2d 665 (1987).

McDonald v. University of Illinois, 375 F. Supp. 95 (1974). Affirmed by 503 F.2d 105.

Gorman v. University of Rhode Island, 837 F.2d 7 (1988).

Texas Medical School v. Than, 901 S.W.2d 926 (1995).

Garrity v. New Jersey, 385 U.S. 493 (1967).

Furutani v. Ewigleben, 297 F. Supp. 1163 (1969).

Baxter v. Palmigiano, 425 U.S. 308 (1976).

Morale v. Grigel, 422 F. Supp. 988 (1976).

Hardison v. Florida A&M University, 706 So. 2d 111 (1998).

U.S. v. Miami University, 294 F.3d 797 (2002).

FIRE's *GUIDES* TO
STUDENT RIGHTS ON CAMPUS
BOARD OF EDITORS

Vivian Berger – Vivian Berger is the Nash Professor of Law Emerita at Columbia Law School. Berger is a former New York County Assistant District Attorney and a former Assistant Counsel to the NAACP Legal Defense and Educational Fund. She has done significant work in the fields of criminal law and procedure (in particular, the death penalty and habeas corpus) and mediation, and continues to use her expertise in various settings, both public and private. She and her late husband, Professor Curtis J. Berger, are coauthors of "Academic Discipline: A Guide to Fair Process for the University Student," published in the *Columbia Law Review* (volume 99). Berger is General Counsel for and a National Board Member of the American Civil Liberties Union and has written numerous essays and journal articles on human rights and due process.

T. Kenneth Cribb, Jr. – T. Kenneth Cribb, Jr. is the President of the Intercollegiate Studies Institute, a nonpartisan, educational organization dedicated to furthering the American ideal of ordered liberty on college and university campuses. He served as Counselor to the Attorney General of the United States and later as Assistant to the

President for Domestic Affairs during the Reagan administration. Cribb is also President of the Collegiate Network of independent college newspapers. He is former Vice Chairman of the Fulbright Foreign Scholarship Board.

Alan Dershowitz – Alan Dershowitz is the Felix Frankfurter Professor of Law at the Harvard Law School. He is an expert on civil liberties and criminal law and has been described by *Newsweek* as "the nation's most peripatetic civil liberties lawyer and one of its most distinguished defenders of individual rights." Dershowitz is a frequent public commentator on matters of freedom of expression and of due process, and is the author of eighteen books, including, most recently, *Why Terrorism Works: Understanding the Threat, Responding to the Challenge*, and hundreds of magazine and journal articles.

Paul McMasters – Paul McMasters is the First Amendment Ombudsman at the Freedom Forum in Arlington, Virginia. He speaks and writes frequently on all aspects of First Amendment rights, has appeared on various television programs, and has testified before numerous government commissions and congressional committees. Prior to joining the Freedom Forum, McMasters was the Associate Editorial Director of *USA Today*. He is also past National President of the Society of Professional Journalists.

Edwin Meese III - Edwin Meese III holds the Ronald Reagan Chair in Public Policy at the Heritage Foundation. He is also Chairman of Heritage's Center for Legal and Judicial Studies. Meese is a Distinguished Visiting Fellow at the Hoover Institution at Stanford University, and a Distinguished Senior Fellow at The University of London's Institute of United States Studies. He is also Chairman of the governing board at George Mason University in Virginia. Meese served as the 75th Attorney General of the United States under the Reagan administration.

ABOUT FIRE

FIRE's mission is to defend, sustain, and restore individual rights at America's colleges and universities. These rights include freedom of speech, legal equality, due process, religious liberty, and sanctity of conscience—the essential qualities of civil liberty and human dignity. FIRE's core goals are to protect the unprotected against repressive behavior and partisan policies of all kinds, to educate the public about the threat to individual rights that exists on our campuses, and to lead the way in the necessary and moral effort to preserve the rights of students and faculty to speak their minds, to honor their consciences, and to be treated honestly, fairly, and equally by their institutions.

FIRE is a charitable and educational tax-exempt foundation within the meaning of Section 501 (c) (3) of the Internal Revenue Code. Contributions to FIRE are deductible to the fullest extent provided by tax laws. FIRE is funded entirely through individual donations; we receive no government funding. Please visit **www.thefire.org** for more information about FIRE.

FIRE

KNOW YOUR RIGHTS PROGRAM:
FIRE's *GUIDES* TO STUDENT RIGHTS ON CAMPUS PROJECT

FIRE believes it imperative that our nation's future leaders be educated as members of a free society, able to debate and resolve peaceful differences without resort to repression. Toward that end, FIRE implemented its pathbreaking *Guides* to Student Rights on Campus Project.

The creation and distribution of these *Guides* is indispensable to challenging and ending the climate of censorship and enforced self-censorship on our college campuses, a climate profoundly threatening to the future of this nation's full enjoyment of and preservation of liberty. We trust that these *Guides* will enable a wholly new kind of discourse on college and university campuses.

A distinguished group of legal scholars serves as Board of Editors to this series. The board, selected from across the political and ideological spectrum, has advised FIRE on each of the *Guides*. The diversity of this board proves that liberty on campus is not a question of partisan politics, but of the rights and responsibilities of free individuals in a society governed by the rule of law.

It is our liberty, above all else, that defines us as human beings, capable of ethics and responsibility. The struggle for liberty on American campuses is one of the defining struggles of the age in which we find ourselves. A nation that does not educate in freedom will not survive in freedom and will not even know when it has lost it. Individuals too often convince themselves that they are caught up in moments of history that they cannot affect. That history, however, is made by their will and moral choices. There is a moral crisis in higher education. It will not be resolved unless we choose and act to resolve it. We invite you to join our fight.

Please visit **www.thefire.org/guides** for more information on FIRE's *Guides* to Student Rights on Campus.

CONTACTING FIRE
www.thefire.org

Send inquiries, comments, and documented instances of betrayals of free speech, individual liberty, religious freedom, the rights of conscience, legal equality, due process, and academic freedom on campus to:

Submissions via website preferred

FIRE's website:
www.thefire.org

By email:
fire@thefire.org

By mail:
601 Walnut Street, Suite 510
Philadelphia, PA 19106

By phone/fax:
215-717-FIRE (3473) (phone)
215-717-3440 (fax)

AUTHORS

Harvey A. Silverglate, co-founder and chairman of the Board of Directors of the Foundation for Individual Rights in Education, is a lawyer, journalist, lecturer, and writer who has specialized in civil liberties and criminal defense work since 1967. Mr. Silverglate is the coauthor, with Alan Charles Kors, of *The Shadow University: The Betrayal of Liberty on America's Campuses*.

Josh Gewolb is a graduate of Harvard College and served as a Program Officer at FIRE's Boston office from 2002-2003. In 2006, he graduated Magna Cum Laude from the University of Michigan Law School and currently works for Debevoise & Plimpton, a law firm in New York City.